Do You Realize?

First published by O Books, 2010
O Books is an imprint of John Hunt Publishing Ltd., The Bothy, Deershot Lodge, Park Lane, Ropley,
Hants, SO24 0BE, UK
office1@o-books.net
www.o-books.net

Distribution in:	South Africa
	Stephan Phillips (pty) Ltd
UK and Europe	Email: orders@stephanphillips.com
Orca Book Services	Tel: 27 21 4489839 Telefax: 27 21 4479879
orders@orcabookservices.co.uk	
Tel: 01202 665432 Fax: 01202 666219	Text copyright Marion Steel 2009
Int. code (44)	
	Design: Stuart Davies
USA and Canada	
NBN	ISBN: 978 1 84694 330 0
custserv@nbnbooks.com	
Tel: 1 800 462 6420 Fax: 1 800 338 4550	All rights reserved. Except for brief quotations
	in critical articles or reviews, no part of this
Australia and New Zealand	book may be reproduced in any manner without
Brumby Books	prior written permission from the publishers.
sales@brumbybooks.com.au	
Tel: 61 3 9761 5535 Fax: 61 3 9761 7095	The rights of Marion Steel as author have been
	asserted in accordance with the Copyright,
Far East (offices in Singapore, Thailand,	Designs and Patents Act 1988.
Hong Kong, Taiwan)	
Pansing Distribution Pte Ltd	
kemal@pansing.com	A CIP catalogue record for this book is available
Tel: 65 6319 9939 Fax: 65 6462 5761	from the British Library.

Printed by Digital Book Print

The author and publisher wish to thank the following for permission to quote from
copyrighted material:

'I know you', from SELECTED POEMS AND PROSE OF PAUL CELAN by Paul Celan, translated by John Felstiner. Copyright
© 2001 by John Felstiner. Used by permission of W.W. Norton & Company, Inc and Suhrkamp Verlag Berlin.

'Youth' by Octavio Paz, translated by Charles Tomlinson, from COLLECTED POEMS OF OCTAVIO PAZ 1957-1987,
copyright © 1968 by Octavio Paz and Charles Tomlinson. Reprinted by permission of New Directions Publishing Corp
and Pollinger Limited.

'Maithuna' by Octavio Paz, translated by Eliot Weinberger, from COLLECTED POEMS OF OCTAVIO PAZ 1957-1987,
copyright © 1986 by Octavio Paz and Eliot Weinberger. Reprinted by permission of New Directions Publishing Corp
and Pollinger Limited.

'The Hollow Men', 'The Waste Land' and 'Burnt Norton' by T.S. Eliot, from COLLECTED POEMS OF T.S.ELIOT 1909-
1962, copyright © 1963 by T.S. Eliot. Reprinted by permission of Faber and Faber Ltd.

Excerpts from THE DUINO ELEGIES AND THE SONNETS TO ORPHEUS by Rainer Maria Rilke, translated by A. Poulin, Jr.
copyright © 1975, 1976, 1977 by A. Poulin, Jr. Reprinted by permission of Houghton Mifflin Harcourt Publishing
Company.
All rights reserved.

Do You Realize?

A Story of Love and Grief
and the Colours of Existence

Marion Steel

BOOKS

Winchester, UK
Washington, USA

To S,

and to N:

*'And if the earthly has forgotten
you, say to the still earth: I flow.
To the rushing water speak: I am.'*

CONTENTS

'The night is my nudity
The stars are my teeth
I throw myself among the dead
Dressed in white sunlight'

Georges Bataille, *The Impossible*

I wish to thank all those who appear in these pages, whilst acknowledging that every story from a life can only be a fragment, and even if seeking to attain some kind of truth, necessarily in its construction becomes a fiction.

PART I

'Yearning is the umbilical cord of living.'

Søren Kierkegaard, *Journals*

Mina

The other day, as I came out from the station, I caught a glimpse of dark hair and, for a second, I thought it was you, Mina.

It wasn't the first time. Sometimes it feels like if I could only will it hard enough, you will reappear. Sometimes I think that I am still trying to hold you in the world because I know how much you didn't want to leave it.

I have decided to call you Mina. It has an echo of your real name within it. But now, as I write this, I realize that the first letter of Mina is M. And on the heels of that thought, comes the realization that all the letters of the name I have given you are contained within my own.

We did not look the same. You were dark, and I have light hair. It is true that you were small, like me, thin like me - only you were much thinner. From the time I first met you, I knew that there were many overlaps that made me feel particularly connected to you: we were close in age, and there were many uncanny similarities in our life histories, and in our situation.

When I heard of your death, first of all, I was shocked. It was the middle of August. I had just come back from my summer holiday, I turned on my computer, and it was the first email I saw. I opened it. And my heart jumped into my mouth, Mina. It told me you had died the week before. Yet I carried on with my day, much as usual. I saw my patients, attended meetings, I even ate my lunch, in front of my computer screen, as I was accustomed to do. But deep down inside of me something had locked. The day passed. I went home in the evening at the usual time. I went to bed. Then, I remember, I woke suddenly in the night, I was sweating, and my heart was beating fast. That's when the freefall started. After that, I didn't see any further patients for a month. In fact, for weeks, I barely left my house.

For a while, it was like I too dropped out of the world. Although, in my case, I took myself out of it. Maybe, deep down, I was questioning my right to belong in it.

You intrigued me from the beginning, Mina. In fact, I think I was more than a little mesmerized by you. You looked so young, sitting there on the hospital bed, with your long dark hair hanging down on each side of your face, like curtains. You were wearing a T-shirt, it revealed that your arms were stick-thin. I must confess I was shocked, although I thought I disguised it. But, later, I came to know how you noticed such things. That first time I saw you, you were wearing a nasal feed. Never flattering, I guess the tube seemed all the more intrusive on you because you had such a beautiful face. Dark eyes, olive skin, long lashes that framed your stare as you took me in. You looked at me as you spoke, but your answers were monosyllabic, in response to my questioning.

I remember that your lunch arrived. And how we both looked at it, but neither of us said anything. Then you told me about the chemo. How you had been unable to tolerate it. The vomiting had made you weak, and your body weight had plummeted. And Mina, I knew, when I looked into your eyes, that you had allowed it to.

You left the hospital later that day, the next I heard was that you could no longer tolerate the feeding tube, and the little weight you had gained, in the hospital, was beginning to fall away...

Two weeks later, when you came back to see me, your sister brought you in a wheelchair. I remember that your eyes were downcast, your voice, low in any case, was barely there. That day, I questioned you about your eating, and you got sparky with me. You reported how you had tried to eat some fish and chips - unsuccessfully. I began to visualize strong-tasting, soft and colourful foods that might slip down the throat more easily. I remember I mentioned smoked salmon and avocado, prawns in garlic. And suddenly, you laughed, as you told me how you often used to eat those very foods when you were single – so easy to eat, you said, so easy to prepare.

And so Mina, we laid out these foods between us, and in all their colours they appeared before us – the palest green, within the deep dark greenness of the enclosing skin, the brightest orange, followed by the palest pink. We became more and more animated, reminiscing, and gorging ourselves. We had a feast. And we laughed a lot.

At the end of the session, you said that your taste buds had been re-awakened. You were going to ask your sister to take you to the supermarket right away. And, you were laughing as you said it.

I have thought many times since of that session and of the food we tasted together and how we laughed so freely...

And, so, eventually, Mina, you told me about your life. How your mother left when you were still a child. How you decided to be a mother to your two younger sisters. You grew up asserting a fierce independence, for your father's love placed a strain on you. As soon as you could, you flew. You had your friends, a job that absorbed you, your flat was your sanctuary, you could always escape to. You kept men at a distance from you.

Until, one day, you met someone new. You told me how it was like opening the secret door onto a beautiful garden. You contemplated another life, even children.

Then came the diagnosis. And suddenly, like in a dream, the beautiful garden faded out of view. As did you. With the treatment, you watched your weight take a downward slide, and it came clearly to you what you had to do. You would not allow the disease to have its way with you. You would just slip gently out of life. You did not want a slow deterioration, a painful death. You did not want to lose control. And yet, as your body shut down and the delusions and the paranoia took hold, suddenly you were afraid, you were lost, and there was nothing for you to hold on to. Then it seemed like everyone was against you. You would not go into hospital. Yet, without your family's insistence, it seems you would have died. Later, the nurse told you how your weight had fallen below the cut off point for life.

You were so close to death, you almost touched it. But you did not, as you expected, reach out to embrace it. Suddenly, it had repelled you. Suddenly, it was like Life was calling you. Life had held out its arms towards you and you had run back towards it.

And what was it, I asked, that you had chosen to come back to? And, I remember, Mina, how you looked away, and how the silence and the space between us grew. Then you spoke. Slowly. You spoke about him. How when you had wanted to die, you had waited, impatiently, for him to go. Yet, he did not. You had pushed him away, and yet, he had stayed. This surprised you. And then, suddenly, you said, you knew: it was just as you felt life slipping away from you. Suddenly, it had pierced you through and through

- like an arrow -

       that

          death

             means

                separation.

And you realized that you did not want to be separated...

In our early sessions you talked feverishly about statistics, benchmarks, probabilities, possibilities. You took refuge in rationality, you were trying to figure out your chances. But it seemed like it was Certainty that you were stretching your hands out to.

And there was none. This was probably the most difficult thing. Not knowing.

As the weeks progressed, you told me of the night-time terrors. Waking in the night, sweating and shaking. Thinking there was no hope. Thinking that death was reaching out to you...

In your dreams you were always swimming in a dark sea, blackness all around you, and endless night...

And then, one day, when you came to see me you were calmer. You told me that you were feeling optimistic about the operation that you hoped would cure you. You were hoping to draw a line under the last year, you said that it would be a new beginning, a new life was beckoning to you.

You told me that it was like you were opening again that gate, into the beautiful garden.

You

The last time I saw you, I was in my car. I had just rounded the bend and, suddenly, there you were and we were staring straight at each other. You were walking back from the station, close to the edge of the pavement. You were taking a drag from your cigarette. In the back seat, my son was speaking, I focused on the road ahead, then when I glanced back through my driving mirror, you were gone.

*

When I think of you now, everything seems jumbled up, even a bit chaotic. Everything about you and the times when we were together, the way that you were, the way you spoke, and didn't speak, the way you smiled at me, the things that you said, and didn't say, the way that you glared at me, the tensions, the silences, the gaps between us that emerged at the beginning, but opened up increasingly towards the end – they all flit around my brain, seemingly chaotically, like bees around a honey pot, they swarm around, they swoop down on me out of the deep blue when I least expect them to. They sting me with their sweetness.

*

'Let's go to a hotel,' you said. It was the first – no the second - time we went out. I was taken aback. You surprised me. Earlier that evening, there had been some moments when we sat in silence, we just looked at each other, and neither of us said anything. You took my hand and looked at it. Then you looked back at me. And still we did not speak. You know, I was surprised then. It did not feel like you wanted to possess me, just that you looked and saw me.

Later, we left the bar. We walked along the main street. As we turned into a side road, you touched my face.

I remember the sudden feel of your mouth, the darkness, together with the strangest sensation of falling, stars, your tight embrace.

Then I was in my car,
Pulling into my driveway

– a sharp turning –

I narrowly missed the gate.

I glanced at my watch.
Felt a rush of apprehension.

I was late.

*

After

I thought of
Nothing

14

So much

As
You

With your eyes closed

The clarity
Of silent heartbeats

After

The beginning,

When you caught me off guard with your clear gaze.

It was like you looked

right
        into
               me.

Yet, strangely, I allowed it. It intrigued me,
Your look of detachment
Interlaced with intimacy…

Seated opposite me,
Visibly relaxed.

Perhaps, I could say, in some ways then,
You were at your best.
(Did you know, I even liked the way you used to cross your

legs...?)
First one way, then the other...

So

     quintessentially

          you

Your gaze, your ways,
Your laugh,
Your impatience,
Your irritation that you sometimes used,
– so it seemed to me –
To form a wall

Between us

Your humour could even be cruel,
Though not towards me

(I'm afraid I have to admit
It was kind of a pastime

Between us

To comment on the foibles
Of others).

*

Do you remember how you used to wait for me on the station platform at the end of the day? I know it was to smoke a cigarette, and yet, every time I saw you catch sight of me, it seemed to me that your eyes danced...

As you touched me
With your glance.

And my heart crept

Then leapt

At the sight of you

(Though I did not show it).

*

And after

With your lips
You entered me

That was
After

Your words

Touched me
With the most gentle caress

– And it is true to say,
I would never have guessed –

That words could become

such delicate

and tender things.

*

Do you remember that night that we walked through the city? A breeze blew from across the river and the water was deep and dark because the tide was full. I remember that we were talking about CGR, of secrets, and of how some secrets are best left unrevealed. As we crossed over the bridge, we caught our breath, as the whole city lay before us.

Earlier that evening, over dinner, you had said how you can never know another person. You were so emphatic, I disputed it, reflexively. But something must have lodged. Something connected, when, later, I remembered CGR's verses: 'For none shall guess the secret of your griefs and fears'.

*

Do you recall that time that we went for lunch in the restaurant on the Fifth Floor? We talked about Sartre's couple: the woman and the man who go out on a dinner date. Sartre tells of how the man takes the woman's hand, yet she pretends not to notice. She begins to laugh more loudly, to talk more quickly, all to cover up the fact that she does not know how to respond. She does not know how to respond because she has not yet made a decision. Sartre tells us the woman is in bad faith. But, it is a fact, it can be difficult to make a decision, can it not? Sometimes it is easiest to prevaricate. To play for time. We all do it. Perhaps Sartre was a little hard on the woman.

*

Once, I remember running through the dark and the rain towards the station. We had been in a bar. We were careless of the rain because we were drunk. It lashed all around us, hitting the puddles furiously, like it was pursuing us, it drove down our faces as we held hands and ran. I remember you caught sight of a bus that had stopped, and you pulled me onto it. The bus was steamy. It was packed. We stood close up together and you reached out to touch my wet hair, and I looked at you and you looked at me, and your face was radiant and your eyes were bright. I don't remember the journey, only your eyes and your face, and that when we got off the bus the rain had stopped, as suddenly as it had begun.

*

Do you remember that night in the garden? It was a hot night. The leaves rustled gently, for the breeze was slight. I remember the softness of the hair on the back of your neck, the feel of your lips, and how the air trembled.

Earlier, you had talked about your father. We were walking back from the bar, through the back streets, to my house I had just bought a few months before. I remember I fumbled with the lock of my front door. I dropped my keys and you bent down to pick them up, and, as you did so you switched to talking about my father, do you remember? You said that he probably loved me too much. Strange how I remember you saying that so well, and how you made a joke of it. 'So much that he did not speak to me for two years,' I answered. Maybe my voice shook a little as I said it, but my tone was light. We went inside.

'I am like your father,' you replied. I remember how you looked at me as you said it. Yet I denied it.

'Why would you want me?' you asked me. And for a moment I could not think of how to respond. We were sitting in the garden, the leaves were whispering all around us. They leant forward and caressed us, as the heat embraced us. Then I embraced you.

*

Sometimes, there have been nights, as I am falling asleep,

Closing my eyes,

I see

A boy lingering in the dark, on the stair.

Listening, body tensed, alert: waiting –

For what, unknowing
How to be

You know, it is the strangest thing, how sometimes it seems to
me that your memories, are my memories, it is like I was

There.

I listen, and it is as if I can hear two hearts beating.

*

You. And me.

It was like something shifted,
magically.

I remember the moment when you first really looked at me,
That moment that
stretched.....................

Like it could survive infinity

and, do you know, it was like, from that point on,
I felt free.

You seemed fearless,
And you encouraged me.

*

That first summer slipped quickly into winter. There was the
night that we sat on the cold step.

'Go on, just leave me,' I said. We had come out of the restaurant,
you were striding ahead. You paused, retraced your steps. 'We
can't sit there,' you said.

Then you sat down beside me and the tension just went.

Later, that same night, we sat on a bench in the square.

It was a clear, cold night close to Christmas and the lights in the trees were blinking and winking at us, like stars that had shot out of the sky and secretly landed there.

*

(That same night, you had taken me to see a play,
About a man who invited himself to stay,
In the house of a family –

They were not exactly a happy family
But they were getting along,
Making the best of things –

This man did not behave well,
There was deception
And misconception

But it was not only him –
I am sure you can guess,

By implication –

And yet, he was the spark
That blew

The family apart.)

*

Do you remember the time that I texted you
'Sorry, I can't do this'

It was the middle of the night

I had just returned
And looked at my son, sleeping

The next day
You looked

At me

And did not speak

Your eyes
Like bullets

After

On a clear winter's day, we took ourselves off

To see an exhibition.

Inside the gallery, we saw thoughts
Translated into reconstructed rooms,
Alongside images
Of the artist,

Recorded, when he was alive,
In his trademark hat...

Then colossal stones, intersecting,
Sheets of metal,
Iron rods,
Zinc
And blocks of fat

Predominating

All declaring loudly the solidity of their existence...

You, I noticed, were attentive to that

Ineluctable modality of the visible...
snotgreen, bluesilver, rust: coloured signs. Limits of the diaphane.

And then,
Suddenly

We came upon the vitrines.

I was silent. Mesmerized.

You
Were slightly amused,
I think,
By the degree

To which these disparate things
Held me.

These fragments: of felt, fat, cloth, black copper, a honey comb,
twigs and grasses, and between them scraps of paper inscribed in
black ink...

Signatures of all things,

Only traces,

And yet, to me, contained behind the glass, they seemed to offer
some kind of whole

presence.

Later, I saw you stop behind one glass case

It was an empty suit...

You were ahead of me
You waited for me to catch up

And we stood...

It was like looking in a mirror,
Without a face

No place

To go

After

We went to the bar, and talked of other things...

*

'You know, I have not felt this way...'
Your voice trailed, then you resumed,

'...in over twenty years.'

You looked at me.

Then 'Perhaps never, ' reached me clearly through the fug of
smoke and beer.

It was like you were voicing something that was uncertain,
And yet...

There was a finality in the way you said it.

It was early evening and we were in a crowded bar. The disco
beat was rising.

Someone had turned up the volume.

I leaned forward to catch your next words, yet heard only

'can't'

Then

'again'.

I was staring at your face, but then you were getting up,

'Come on,'

You seemed suddenly impatient: 'It's nearly time for the next train.'

It seemed to me we had scarcely begun
Yet there you were, gesturing irritably,

'It's too late,' you said.
'You don't want to be late for your son.'

*

Do you know, the first time we met on the train I was not even remotely physically attracted to you. We talked, passed the time, since we found ourselves on the same train, it was the polite thing to do. To be honest, I was even a little bored by you.

I changed my hours. Months went by. Then there you were that winter's morning, when I got on at the station. The train was late because the world was frozen. I don't know why I began to tell you about *A Dialogue on Love*. I had just been reading it. The writer, Eve Sedgwick, was an American queer theorist and poet – maybe I thought that would appeal to you. It was an account of her analysis. You seemed intrigued, so I lent it to you. (Though afterwards, you remarked that you didn't like the poetry, that it did nothing for you.) Then a few months later, in a café, you handed me a book by an Italian author – *Don't Move* – it was later made into a film with Penelope Cruz. A story about a woman and a man, who fall into a relationship, she loves him, and he loves her, but then he is too afraid, he is cruel, he leaves her, later he returns. In the end, she dies.

*

We texted a lot. Once I sent you a short text to tell you that everything had changed. I followed it up with a letter in which I tried to explain. The letter was long. In fact, it took me a month to write. I wrote it in the day and I wrote it in the night. It was long, but clear-cut - or so I thought. You read it. Then you asked me to meet you, in a café, as we used to do. I resisted at first, but I always found it difficult to say no to you. I don't deny that it would have been hard for me to end it with you. But, the point is, it was not beyond me, then.

*

A long time after that (at least a couple of years) you sent me a text that said, 'Everything changes'. I was outraged, I just could not contain my anger towards you. We texted furiously for hours, and into the night. Then, in the early hours, I woke up crying and laughing at the same time. It seems you had that

effect on me.
(With you, I always laughed – eventually.)

*

Once, I told you how I like to get to the end of things. I forget now what it was that led me to say this, but I remember how you smiled at me, wryly. I remember your smile because it was so familiar to me, and also, it made me realize immediately what it was I had said. Of course, you followed it up with a comic riposte, which was lost on me, as we were just getting off the train and the signal for the doors was beeping. In fact, it was the last time that we met (although I didn't know it then). We had arranged to see each other the next day. Then you cancelled. Then, a week later, you sent me those terrible texts.

*

So how can I begin

To sum up all the pleasures

Of all the days
And all your ways

To sum up:

You?

You...

Who when you looked at me, that night:
You know the night, I mean

It was like

You

Saw right
Through

To the heart of me

And I remind myself
That in the beginning,

It was you,
It was you,

Who was
As some might say, to put it simply

keen...

       on

                me.

You

Who wanted everything
(Do you remember half of what you said?)

To put it bluntly,

It was

You

Who told me you could give me whatever I wanted
Pleasure-wise

(You practically boasted –
and I know it is not just inside my head).

One could even say you were pretty arrogant
(given the situation).

Really there's no getting away from it…
(Let's not pretend).

Although I do not exclude myself

(I was proud,
and yet,
there were,

spiralling,

tendrils of guilt

wrapped
around

my elation.)

And now, you might say I am angry –
And yes, maybe,

(I guess it is true)

But really
I am just exasperated

– And crushed –

At the loss of you.

*

You said the strangest things, like they weren't strange at all.

Once you told me that
        I
                ate
                      men
                          up.

Although actually, when I stop to recall,

It wasn't exactly that –
No, not that at all,

Rather,
you said that I

chewed
men up and then
        spat
           them
              out.

You even laughed when you said it, like you had said nothing surprising or unpleasant. In fact, it took a moment for me to realize what it was you had said.

And then, you were speaking of other things, and I missed the moment to ask you exactly what it was you had meant.

I reminded you of it later but you pretended to be nonplussed. But it happened. You said it.

You were there.

So then, beware

I rise with my long red hair
And I eat men like air.

*

Another time you told me that men hovered round me
Like bees round a honey pot.

We were standing on the platform at the time, and the train was just coming in.

You were laughing, as you said it,
And I did not comment.

(To tell you the truth
I was not sure what to answer.

Or whether it was better to respond or not.)

*

That was the summer,
In the late afternoons in an Italian garden,
Sheltered from the heat within the ancient city wall,

It seemed to me that all the trees
Were whispering to me

Your name.

And that you came

In my thoughts...

But down on the beach, there was only the sun's fierce glare.

On my return, you greeted me, casually, like you didn't care.

Strange then
To remember your lips

in my hair.

Your lips
On
My lips

Back at your place

The lips of your night
damp hollows
unborn
echoes

Barely touching, you moaned gently, when you came, close, to me, like you dare not, could not, would not go there, like you were afraid,

To hear two hearts beating
Like one heartbeat
Like one

Like

unborn echoes...

That's when you left me.

That time I found you outside, in your garden. You told me to leave, then you walked me home.

You went back alone.

*

Once – it was some time after – you told me, how still you found
strands of my hair...

upon your chair...

You were smiling, so I laughed – affecting nonchalance –
In other words, I lied.

It is not possible, I said,
For them still to be there

After all this time.

(But later, you know, I cried.)

*

I knew what you were communicating to me,

Before I died.

Unborn echoes

Or do I mean,

Before I was born.

You knew,
Before the essence

Before the descent...

The shadow
Behind

A life
Not lived.

*

That day when I met you in September, the heat of the summer stretched out between us, yet, you greeted me coolly, like a stranger, do you remember? You were wearing dark sunglasses and I could not see your eyes. The restaurant was empty. We made our way to the small courtyard at the back, and seated ourselves under the umbrellas. We ordered wine by the glass. Your food was high carb, mine was a salad.

You talked about work. You were edgy and distant. Eventually, I ran out of patience: I asked you a direct question and you responded with irritation. Then, as always, I pushed: 'I just don't understand you,' I said. And then: 'Maybe we should just end here and now!'

'OK,' you said. In fact, you even added something like it was a good idea. Then you sat back in your seat and looked at me through your sunglasses.

I looked down at my plate, at this huge white expanse, with just a few sad, green leaves upon it. Then, placing my knife and fork carefully on either side of the leaves (to show I had not finished) I got up from the table. I was upset. I was crying. Then I remember I said the first thing that came into my head. It was something about feeling left.

When I returned, I remember that something had shifted. The gap had closed up. You looked across at me, you said something and we both laughed. I ate the green leaves. Strangely, things seemed as they had always been. You asked me about my patient, 'the one that died' and I told you everything.

Later, you said that you could not comprehend your earlier reaction. Later still, I laughingly said, 'But of course, you are finished with me!' And we both laughed some more.

But we never spoke about it afterwards, because after that day the gap opened up even more than before.

*

I have never liked gaps. I was a child who was scared of the gaps in the pavement. Not the lines, but those fissures and cracks that tripped you up, because you never knew they were there.

In my life I know that I like to seek out the links, I strain for connections. For are we not all links in the chain, and could you not say that everything connects with everything else, in some way or another – don't you think?

Certainly, the things that preoccupy us often seem to converge, and then merge, one into the other. It's an ever-expanding circle.

And yet, in my case, sometimes the circle contracts, and I am caught in the vortex. My thoughts spiral in and tighten their grip on me, I am caught in the downward draft and then it feels like I will never be free.

And yet, from when I was a child, I discovered that if I could put my thoughts into words then it was like – how can it put it? –

Perhaps, I can say, it was like

my thoughts could fly away

from me.

Words

'Words are not real.'

That's what you once wrote to me. It was one of your last texts. You knew that would get to me. Certainly, it brought me up short.

Despite their inherent contradiction, those words jolted me.

'But, words are everything to me,' was what I thought.

On reflection, I realized that I felt this way because words fill much of my life, or, perhaps, more accurately, I fill my life with words.

As a psychotherapist, I work with words all the time. Words and the spaces between them...

*

We now know that a baby hears our voices from within the womb, that it is already familiar with its mother's voice before birth.

The baby hears words before it even enters into the world.

The baby looks into its mother's face and hears her voice and within the first months can begin to respond to gestures and words with similar sounds.

And so, we come into being through the words of others.

*

As a child, I was aware of how my life was like a story to me: sometimes it seemed as if I lived in order to tell it. At school, I was outgoing with my friends: I liked to speak, to entertain, I joked around a lot. But I was also a solitary child. I liked to shut myself in secret places because I liked to dream, and I wrote a lot.

All my speaking and all my writing was, perhaps, a search for some kind of definition. Like a child with drawing paper tracing an image, I liked to trace over my reality with words, and I found that in that way, what seemed otherwise indistinct could then take on a more definite form and become more visible to me.

*

One day, when I was not yet eight years old, my cat disappeared. At first, I called for her, I went looking, and then I waited, but she did not reappear. Gradually, over the days that then stretched into weeks and months, all my hoping gave way to an empty desolation.

So I grieved through my words: in poems and stories, some of which I have still.

When I conjured up words it seemed her absence, which was otherwise invisible, took on a visibility.

And so, I re-called her, and in this way, she continued to have a presence for me.

Without words I think that perhaps my grief would have remained in some way intangible to me.

Yet, through words I could reach out and touch it... Grasp it...

It was like my words formed a bridge, for me to cross over the abyss.

*

Now, I see beneath my grief for my cat, there lay the shadow of other losses. The year before, when I was seven, my grandmother, who lived with us, went to sleep one night and never woke up. Six weeks later, equally suddenly and unexpectedly, my grandfather had a heart attack; he was admitted to hospital and died a few days later.

When my mother told me, I cried.

'Everybody dies,' I said.

We were in my parents' bedroom; I flung myself down onto their bed and buried my head in the pillows.

I remember the words in my head. They were angry, bitter words that repeated over and over. They were the only words that came to me:

'Nobody can make it better.'

They filled my head and I could hear nothing else.

And I remember a desperate feeling: like a kind of falling...

It was not entirely unfamiliar to me...

Yet I could not speak...

Maybe I was too young then, for words to hold me in their embrace.

*

In his book, *Inner Experience*, the philosopher Georges Bataille wrote: 'We are nothing, neither you nor I, beside burning words which could pass from me to you, imprinted on a page: for I would only have lived in order to write them, and, if it is true that they are addressed to you, you will live from having had the strength to hear them.'

Do we not all exist through our words, through our communication with each other?

Certainly, our words will continue to exist beyond our physical living in the world.

Alive, or even dead, we are all links in the chain, connecting up with each other. In this way we are all in the lives of others.

I am giving you something of my life, something of me, in these words that I offer to you and you, in turn are living them now as you read them...

*

I live to speak and to be heard, yet these words that I am writing, are both my own and other people's, intermingling. My words arise out of theirs. For everything that I have heard and read is there in the kaleidoscope of my thinking.

So it is that we assimilate the thoughts and words of others, and in so doing, something new emerges as we make them our own.

I like to think that this is what occurs in therapy, for the client, but also for the therapist.

*

And yet, finally, it has to be said, words are not everything. Certainly, around death there is a silence.

I remember how my grandmother's skin was cold when I kissed her the last time. I remember thinking: she will never wake up, nor will she ever speak to me again.

It seemed clear to me then that it was words, or the absence of them, that cut off the dead from the living.

Confronted by death, by silence, words can seem insufficient and paltry things...

But for me, these paltry words are like a rope bridge flung over the ravine, when the gaps between the ropes feel so wide, and I can scarcely reach from one to the other, and I am afraid of falling...

The Goblins

It was some time after my grandmother died, when I came across all her books in our garage. We had recently moved house. I don't remember now what I was doing there that day, possibly getting my bike or my roller skates, when, suddenly, seeing that the car had gone, I glanced over and saw there all the familiar spines, on the back wall.

Instantly, it flashed into my head, myself on a little stool, seated at my grandmother's feet some years before. (She was severely arthritic and could barely leave her room, so I would often go and knock on her door.) She would tell me stories; she was kind but stern. She told me how important it was for me to go to school and learn. And, always, my gaze would fall on her old and dusty books, that looked like they had been there for a hundred years or more.

After this discovery, of their new resting place, I would spend long hours in my father's garage, reading my grandmother's books, seated on the stool (which I found in the corner), as before. (It seemed that she had been an excellent pupil, for inside the flyleaf of each one of her childhood books I found, inscribed in black ink: Awarded to Alice Goodman. 1901, 1902, 1903, 1904...)

One of my favourites was *The Child's Companion:* inside there were many black and white illustrations of faraway places and detailed drawings from the natural world. I remember a picture that covered an entire page: it was of a dead bird lying in the snow.

Beneath the drawing, the words:

The Gift of God is Eternal Life.

I remember looking carefully at the bird and trying to ascertain if its eyes were open or closed.

It was hard to tell.

However, one day, a small white book with gold lettering on the cover caught my eye: *Goblin Market* by Christina G Rossetti. Inside I was surprised to find just one long poem. There were pictures, however: coloured illustrations of beautiful, languorous women. I remember gazing at the deep greens and blues and reds of the Pre-Raphaelite paintings, which were magically revealed when you lifted the thin tracing paper that obscured them. The book was delicate but exquisite.

The poem 'Goblin Market' tells of two sisters, Laura and Lizzie. And how, out one day by the brook, they come across goblins calling out their wares: so many delicious, mouth-watering orchard fruits:

> *Apples and quinces,*
> *Lemons and oranges,*
> *Plump unpecked cherries,*
> *Melons and raspberries,*
> *Bloom-down-cheeked peaches,*
> *Swart-headed mulberries,*
> *Wild free-born cranberries,*
> *Crab-apples, dewberries,*
> *Pine-apples, blackberries,*
> *Apricots, strawberries; –*

From this day on, morning and evening, the two sisters hear the goblins' cries: 'Come buy, come buy!'

One evening, Laura lingers, whilst her dutiful sister returns home. In the twilight, she lingers by the brook, alone. She wishes to taste the fruits, yet has no money to pay. The goblins tell her that they will accept the gold upon her head – just one lock of golden hair, and then the fruits will be hers, they say. With a tear in her eye, Laura clips off and hands over the lock, then sucks at the honeyed fruits with a feverish delight until her lips are sore. She takes her fill, until she can eat no more. Back at the house, her sister is waiting for her and greets her at the gate, upbraids her for being so late.

Laura wakes the next morning and drifts through the day as if in a dream. When the sun sets, consumed by her burning desire for more fruits, she returns impatiently to the brook – but the goblins are nowhere to be seen.

Laura loiters and waits, listening for the goblins' cries, and straining to hear. Then, as darkness is descending, her sister begs her to come promptly; for the fruit-call has reached her and she knows they are near.

When Laura realizes this she feels a sudden fear. Her heart contracts, turns cold as stone. Yet she stays there, lingering and alone. Hearing no sound in the silence, she realizes it anew: the goblins have gone, and with their fruits... And so, the dream fades out of view...

Laura becomes more listless with every passing day. She cannot eat, and she is shrinking and fading, even her hair is thinning and turning grey.

Seeing her sister dwindling, 'knocking at Death's door', Lizzie feels there is nothing left to her but to go in search of the goblins, as Laura did before. When she finds them, they come to her, quickly and eagerly, pressing their fruits upon her, more and more. She remains there, her mouth firmly closed, as they push and shove their fruits at her, attempting to get them in, smearing them upon her face, until the juices run down her chin. Eventually, angry and frustrated, they leave her be, and Lizzie runs back home, calls to Laura to suck the juices from her fruit-stained lips… But the fruits are bitter-tasting, and Laura falls to the ground in a deathlike swoon.

Her sister sits by her, meanwhile, through the night, as Laura's pulse flags, fearing that she is drifting out of life. Until the morning comes, and Laura awakes with a smile.

So Lizzie braves the goblins, for the sake of her sister, and defeats them. She is able to take home the fruits upon her own lips, and to save her sister with a kiss.

You could say that 'Goblin Market' is a poem about the perils of temptation and desire: it is a cautionary tale which explores the dangers inherent in wanting and daring too much.

In the poem, desire, once sated, can only lead to loss.

Yearning and mourning, Laura dwindles and begins to pine away…

The poem asks a question:

Pleasure past and anguish past,
Is it death or is it life?

If pleasure and anguish are past, if we lose our desire which both enraptures and torments us, what is left? Life or death?

The poem opts for life. It is love that conquers all, through love, life defeats death.

But the love celebrated at the poem's end is that of a sister: steadfast, resilient and, above all, chaste.

Dream and Life

The leap of the wave
                              whiter
each hour
                    greener
each day
                    younger
death

Octavio Paz

I returned to my work at the hospital in September. It was a month after Mina died.

P was an artist and I was looking at an image that he had just handed to me.

I looked and saw a black circle surrounded by white triangles, followed by a white circle surrounded by black triangles. In each picture, the triangles were positioned at different angles around the void. P was standing next to me over by the window where I had moved to catch the fading light. I was looking into the void but he directed my attention towards the sharp triangles. 'Like glass shattering', he said. P told me that he had begun the paintings soon after his wife's diagnosis.

I looked closer at the triangles, at their stark forms, as P began to point out to me the complexity of their positions, and their precise relationship each to the other, all around the void.

It struck me then how the triangles were framing the void and holding it in place.

Back in our seats, P looked across at me. P had very bushy eyebrows, they overshadowed his eyes which were a prominent blue. Even so, the concentration in his look could feel a little unnerving. On this occasion, I felt my gaze wandering upwards towards his hair which was white, tinged with grey, it was cropped fairly short, but there was lots of it, and perhaps because of this, and the way he dressed in combat trousers, sweatshirts and trainers, P did not look nearly seventy.

My head was full of the paintings. Their after-image hung in the air between us. I remembered how, the week before, he had hesitated on the threshold to my room, glanced at me and nodded, sat in the chair, how he had been slow to speak. He had stumbled to find the words at first, then they had seemed to come all at once, all in a rush, like he had been holding on to them for a long time.

He had told me then of the day that he and his wife had gone to the hospital for the test results. And how afterwards on the bus, neither of them had said that much. It had been after they had got home, as they had stood together looking out of the French windows onto their garden, at the warm spring day, at the vibrant colours of the new flowers, pushing up through the earth, that they had suddenly, almost at the same moment, turned towards each other, clung to each other. They had both cried then.

That had been in April. They had been told that a year, probably, was the maximum that could be hoped for. They were trying to get on with living their lives as best they could, he said, but it was like there was a shadow there between them. It was like there was a hole there at the centre of their existence and neither of them could fill it.

*

A few weeks later, P was speaking about himself and his wife. Time had slipped into another season and the room was darkening as I reached across to switch on the table lamp. The room was warm because the heating was turned high.

P was telling me how he and his wife had both been children of the war. He remembered how once, when he was about four years old, his mother had called him to the window and showed him that the docks were on fire. He remembered the vivid colour of the flames, and how he felt afraid. He recalled that she once took him to see a school nearby soon after it had been bombed. Many of the children and teachers had died.

He remembered too the large eagle on his mantelpiece and how it frightened him. Reflecting on it with me, he thought it seemed somewhat incongruous for a child's bedroom.

P went on to tell me about a recent dream. He was swimming in a dark lake. It was night. He wasn't able to swim very well, and he found that he was going round in circles. Then he realized he had forgotten something: he only had one flipper. He would have to go back for the other. In the dream this felt like an insurmountable task. He pondered over this as he sat there with me. He suggested that perhaps the lake represented his unconscious, that he was unpicking it with me but that he didn't feel very well equipped.

As we neared the end of the session, he told me how he once went diving with his son whilst on vacation. He had never been diving before and had to go for lessons first. Finally, in the last days of their holiday, he had dived around an old shipwreck in the harbour. Prior to doing so he had felt afraid. But he had done it, he had conquered his fear. I connected it with a story that he had told me a few sessions before about how he had once nearly drowned when he got caught underneath a kyak and couldn't release himself. He had described a few long moments of abject terror. And how in that brief time he had felt his death coming up close to him.

That session he had told me of other deaths, sudden and violent, the story of his near-drowning had come near the end. He was shaking as he told me. And I saw the fear on his face, I could taste it. I could feel his fear, and it was mine, too. After he had gone, I had sat in my room, alone, for a long time. But it wasn't just the fear that gripped me and held me. It was my attraction to it.

In this session, however, I was able to reflect with him how in the earlier memory, he had gone under water and got submerged. He became caught up underneath the boat and his fear overcame him, although eventually he surfaced. In this session he had begun with his dream and how he felt ill-equipped, then ended with telling me of how in the past he had sought to overcome his fear and had equipped himself to do so, before diving in the harbour. 'Yes, I overcame myself,' he added, looking at me.

I thought of Nietzsche and the words under and over. And how you have to go under in order to overcome yourself: Thus spoke Zarathustra, 'I say unto you: one must still have chaos in oneself to be able to give birth to a dancing star.'

*

That night, I had a dream. I have had it many times since I was a child, it is very familiar to me.

In the dream, I am always crawling along a narrow bridge which stretches up, into the beyond, as it curves upwards into the sky. I know that down,

below me,

is the ravine.

And as I crawl, the slats of the bridge become ever wider apart, until I am at full stretch to make it from one to the other.

When I look down I saw only the water far beneath me. I have a strong fear of water, and going under – I have a fear, not so much of drowning, as of suffocation...

In the dream I know that that I am precariously balanced. I know that if I lose my nerve, I will fall: for a second this thought freezes me.

Yet, at the same time, I become dimly aware that there are other people making their way behind me: if I stop, they will not make it...

If I get stuck, they will be, too...

This thought pushes me to persevere in my attempt, even though the bridge seems to stretch on into infinity beyond me.

In the dream, I do not know how long I can continue...

But I just keep going...

*

A week or so later, P told me he had dreamed of an eagle. It was trapped inside a tin with its head peering out. He felt sorry for it and wanted to set it free. But when he did so, it just sank to the ground, feebly. Its weakness both surprised and saddened him. He told me that he associated the eagle with nobility, and power. I recalled the eagle on his mantelpiece in his bedroom and how it had instilled fear in him. He elaborated on how as a young child that eagle had seemed to loom so large over him as he lay in his bed at night. This eagle, however, is small. It is he who looms over it as it cowers in its tin. The eagle in his dream is incarcerated and it has lost all its power. It is a pitiful thing.

He then goes on to tell me how he has been thinking a lot about barriers and boundaries. About doors, which can lead to places, and which can shut you out from things. He imagines doors with locks on them. As he speaks, he remembers Kafka's castle and that 'the doorway to nowhere is the most heavily guarded'.

He recalls how in the Kafka story a man stands before the door of the castle and the guard outside tells him: 'It was for you.' However, the door is now barred to him. P breaks down as he tells me, 'He didn't go through it'. He then adds: 'I have spent my life waiting…' The vehemence of his reaction surprises him. He says that the story had never struck him as so poignant before.

As we approach the close of the session, he tells me that he has been re-evaluating his work, and looking again at work he did in the past. He says, 'I probably destroyed work that was OK…' His voice trails off and he looks away from me… And, as he does so, the light from the burning sunset outside my window catches the side of his face for a moment, before the sun sinks down behind the hospital.

*

The next session P tells me how he pondered over his reaction to the Kafka story, which so caught him by surprise. He tells me that he feels he has narrowed down his life, there were choices that were open to him, that he didn't take up. He feels that often he went for the safe option. He regrets this. Now he is nearing the end of his life, he feels a sense of poignancy, of waste. It is like he was waiting for something, but he never knew what it was. He looks at me and sighs.

*

Some months later, P tells me how one day the previous week, he and his wife had woken up to a day of glorious sunshine and they decided on a whim to do something they used to do when they were students. They would spend the day spinning a coin at various points in order to make a decision. And so, he told me, they had given themselves up to a game of chance.

It was a beautiful day, he told me. The spinning of the coin meant that they ended up in a park where they came across a musical performance of Iranian drumming. He told me how he had became drawn in and captivated by the rhythms. How he had been held by the passion of the music and at the same time by its steady control. Whilst listening, he had climbed the heights of intense and exhilarating feelings, all evoked and yet contained within the complex rhythms of the drumming. At one point, close to its end, he had looked at his wife and seen a surprised delight written across her face.

That day, he told me, it was as if everything had been given to them

in the last heat of the sun,
the rise and fall of the music,
that shared glance...

Everything
           released,
                     by a game of chance.

And he smiled,
contemplating,

– so it seemed to me –

the
fragility

of those unanticipated
moments of being.

*

A few sessions later, P presented me with another dream.

He told me how he had woken up and looked out of a window
onto a sea that was so blue, so turquoise, such a colour as he had
never before seen... And he wanted nothing else than to go
rushing out into the water. He wanted to immerse himself in its

currents and to feel the waves on his skin. The dream was so full of colour. The light was bright, the waves so blue and he could see the blinking brightness of the white surf... He felt uplifted...

The dream had been all about getting there. He had encountered obstacles. There had been a lock on a locker that could not be opened. He did not know why he had wanted to open it... Then he had got lost. But, throughout, he had felt he kept within his sight the vision of the sea and the belief that he would get there...

He said that he had felt such joy on awakening...

He went on to tell told me how it has been as if for years, his whole lifetime, he has been waiting for others to come to him, and they never came.

However, more recently, he says he has been reaching out and renewing old contacts. The previous week a couple of people had come to his house, in order to view his work... He is feeling stirred to do new things...

He tells me how, after many years of working in black and white, he is working again in colour...

And he tells me how it is like surfing – you have to know when the big wave comes...

*

It is in the early summer, a few weeks after his dream of the ocean, that P comes to one of our sessions and announces that during the week, he went out and bought some red paint. It is scarlet, he tells me. To go alongside it, he bought a vivid green. He has already begun the painting. White is still there: it is a pure white, almost transparent. And black, 'and all that means', he says, 'it is still there, but only around the fringes'.

In the same session, P speaks of how when he and his wife were first told of her diagnosis, and how far the disease had advanced, a terrible grief had swept over him. From that moment it had felt like his life was ending, along with hers. All he had seen was death and suffering.

Now he says that he feels more focused on life: gradually, he has become aware that she is still living, she is not yet dying. With the passing of time, they are both more tranquil. Death is there, he says, but they are not *in* it, not yet. For now, it has receded more to the fringes, and he tells me how amazing it is to wake up to these mornings when the sunlight coming though the windows is so strong, so bright.

It is so amazing just to feel alive, he says.

PART II

'Between the essence
And the descent
Falls the shadow'

T. S Eliot, 'The Hollow Men'

No Sound Louder

The man sitting before me told me how, a few days earlier, he had been exercising down in the basement of his house. As he concentrated on his body, he had been dimly aware of the movements in the rooms above. He heard the low sound of a radio, then extinguished, followed by the scraping of a chair. Then came the sound of a window being closed. All of this he had registered, but dimly, without really realizing it. It was not until suddenly there was a silence, that he had become instantly alert. His mind left his body, and he was mentally roaming the rooms above, he was listening intently for the smallest sounds. But he heard nothing. The thought skated across his mind: it was like there was nobody there.

He had quickly jumped up and left the basement. Once up the stairs, he passed quickly through the kitchen and opened the door to the sitting room. There was his wife, sitting on the far side of the room, with her back to him, at the computer. She didn't turn round. And he felt a wave of relief, followed by an echo of despair.

It is always there: in the tightness of his chest, he says, like a shadow on the lung...

'I do not think,' he ventures, 'there can be any sound so loud... as that silence...' He falters, 'It is so hard to comprehend it... how it could be... it may not be... many months...' His voice drifts off, then he looks at me, seems to steel himself, to take some resolve: 'I don't know about the future. But for now... she is still here...'

I nod and we look at each other for a few seconds without speaking.

I remember the previous summer. How I stood outside my father's house. I had rung the bell and nobody came.

It must have been my mother who made the phone call. I don't recall now. It seems that I took it in blankly, absorbed the practical implications, then I had jumped in the car, sped down the motorway. All I could think was, to get there.

An hour into the journey, there had been a storm. The rain had slashed down so fast, there had been nothing else to do but take the next exit, and wait for it to pass.

When finally I arrived at my father's house, I left my car at the bottom of the drive, ran up to the front door and rang the bell.

I rang but there was no answer. I rang again. After the sound of the bell died away, the silence that hit me was empty. Clearly, there was nobody there. Glancing round me, I saw how the garden was neglected and overgrown. Beside me, outside the front door, were some old tools and a clapped out lawnmower, the hinge on the gate was broken, it hung there limply, at a kilter, its white paint all but gone. Eight years had passed since my last visit, when it had still seemed like home.

I drove fast to the hospital, thinking: too late. Once inside, I found my father. His face was old and grey. He was all wired up. His voice shook and I had to lean to catch his words as they fell.

His words broke the silence. But they hung there like a shadow between us. It was like we were speaking, without saying anything, and I was wondering and fearing how much longer.......

Into the Night

'And the night, oh the night when the wind
full of outer space gnaws at our faces'

Rainer Maria Rilke, *First Duino Elegy*

'I ask you to follow me step by step into night, better yet, into despair.
I will warn you neither of the holes – you will fall into them – nor of
the walls – you will run up against them. In advance, 'my heart breaks
from laughing' at your awkwardness.'

Georges Bataille, *Inner Experience*

I was dreaming: the dream was red. I remember only a vivid redness and the strongest sensation of warmth and safety. When I woke up, I forgot for a moment I was not a child.

I have an early memory of my father. The image is close up, so much so, in fact, it is only a colour I see – a deep maroon – that I recall so vividly: the colour of my father's jumper, together with its rough texture against my cheek. From this I realize that wrapped within the image is a memory of being held.

My father woke me in the night. I remember still, how it seemed like I jumped up and woke up at the same time. I guess he must have called my name. I seem to remember it penetrating my dream. Or maybe I imagined that, but in any case I heard my father calling. I was waking up and moving swiftly towards him, looking at him, there in the doorway, swaying, and I saw too, the fear in his eyes, at the same time that I registered that he was stuttering, but only one word, one sound repeating, a kind of nonsense coming out of his mouth, like something stuck inside him, like something malfunctioning, like something grotesque, like in a film, like some kind of robot man, except that he was my father and I saw that he could not hold it together and then it was like something seized him, almost as if some force had got hold of him, pushed him from behind and then he fell.

He fell there, right in front of me, and I knelt beside him but looking into his eyes as the sounds kept coming, it was like I saw nothing there.

The ambulance came quickly. Oxygen was applied. And then, back again at the hospital, they said it was a close thing, yet, he would pull through, under their care.

The man told me how he woke in the middle of the night. He woke in a sweat: a terror in his heart. It has happened before, he says, but he just lies there quietly, because he does not want to wake his wife. He knows that it is a terror at what it to come, that together with not knowing.

He tells me that often he just lies in the dark, feeling afraid.

'It is like, here, I can bring, that lonely and dark space in my head, which is there, in the nights,' he says. 'Do you know what I am saying...?'

He is looking at me, to answer.

I am nodding, looking at him, waiting.

'...It is something about not being alone,' he says.

*

The young woman sitting in front of me told me that she woke up in the nights. Fear woke her up. She had thought that she wanted to die, but now she realized she wanted to live.

Sometimes she woke up with a silent scream in her head. It was a scream that nobody heard. Just like the disease, silently destroying her, she said.

She told me that she didn't want to die. Not now, when she had realized that she had so much to live for. And she was still young. How could it be? she said. How could her life stop now, before she had fully lived. Just when she had discovered what it was to live. She wanted to live.

PART III

'On Margate Sands.
I can connect
Nothing with nothing.'

Disconnected

It was the beginning of August when I went off on holiday.

When I returned to work two weeks later it was to the news that my patient, Mina, had died.

I remember that I had just walked through the door. I had switched on my computer, opened my email, and suddenly I was looking at these words written in front of me, and at the same time, there was a sudden heady rush in my ears, like when you go through a tunnel too fast, and I had to sit down, as I was still standing.

I looked down at my diary. Absent-mindedly, I flicked it open to when we were to meet. There was her name, pencilled in. Just as I had written it, a couple of weeks before. I looked at it, as if by looking, it could persuade me that what I had just read was, simply, a terrible mistake. It couldn't be her. She wasn't supposed to die. Her disease was supposed to be curable. *Not her*, I was saying, in my head. *Not her...*

I looked, fixedly, at her name, in my diary, as if, the mere fact of her name being there could magic her back. As if, simply by looking, I could bring about her reappearance, to our session in two days' time.

It was pencilled in because I had been waiting for her to confirm the appointment. She had missed two, before I went away. She had been in a lot of pain. They had put her back on high doses of morphine. She had rung to say that she couldn't make the appointments. Her voice had sounded distant, and faint.

I remember thinking at the time how it sounded like she was barely there.

I looked again at the words and tried to absorb what they were telling me. She had been admitted to her local hospital. They had rediagnosed her. The disease had spread. She and her family had been told it was no longer curable. Then, a few days later, she died.

I had known that she might die. I had known it. But in the abstract.

Her sudden death seemed like a sharp descent, like she had slipped into a freefall out of life.

I realized that I was taken unawares. Was she?

She was only thirty-eight.

Two days later I received a phone call to tell me that someone else I knew had died unexpectedly. She was fifty years old. She had no prior history of heart problems but, one morning, soon after she woke up, her heart just gave out.

Death knows no boundaries. It comes when it comes.

So, there was a death: unexpected.
Then, out of the blue, another.

Then there was

A silence.

The silence
Broke
Me
Up

Like

Nothing

Was

There...

There...

Then

Not

There...

Everything...

closing in.

And then...........

In the night.....

Suddenly

I wake up

Nothing

Pierces
My dreams

I can almost hear it
In the silence

Just as, when I was a child

Nothing

Woke me up

Fear of...

Nothing
Will come
Of nothing

Speak!

Speak! For I hear
Nothing
In all this silence

I cannot speak
My heart is in my mouth

Beating like bats' wings
In my mouth

And I feel
Nothing……..

I cannot speak

……….But fear

It lurks beneath

The silence
Does not speak
To me

A chill
Descending

And I am burning up……

What is it?

Only the silence
And darkness

Falling

Like
When I was a child
In the night
I was afraid
And my mother
Said

It is nothing

Nothing
Will come
Of Nothing

And I could not speak
In the silence.

In the night
I woke up

With my heart
In my mouth

Since I was a child...

Death

Has held me

In its pocket.

Everything closed in.

Disconnected.

In summary: first, there was the silence.

It shouted at me.

Then there were too many words. The words assaulted me. Yet I clung to them. I clung to them because they were something rather than nothing.

Then I fell into a void.

There were no words then. And the silence was empty.

There was nothing there.

The words returned. So many. I would not have believed there could be so many.

I tried to hold onto all these words but they just kept slipping away from me... They made no sense... but they kept coming nonetheless... They would not leave me alone...

But nor did I want to be left...

And then...

The words connected up. The words were in harmony.

I felt such joy, strangely.

There was nothing. Yet something emerged.
How could that be?

To elaborate:

Two deaths, both unexpected.

Then a silence: I was cut off, I was adrift...

Just like when I was a child:

Falling...

For two days I lay in my bed and didn't move. In the night, I slept, fitfully. It was a dreamless, dead sleep. Every time, I woke up, it was to blankness. A terrible blankness. I was all blanked out. It was like I had no thoughts or feelings at all.

Now, I know I had thoughts. But when they came, it was like they came from nowhere.

It was like the thoughts appeared and came at me, like arrows. Wounding me. They passed through me, and left me blank, as before.

They were punitive thoughts. Piercing me. Lacerating me. Perhaps, the blankness was a kind of protection. Perhaps it was better to be totally blank than to have such thoughts.

The thoughts presented themselves as questions, they pierced my mind and, eventually, they became embedded.

Questions like: Why am I alive? Why am I not dead? And, then the thought: It should have been me!

These questions and thoughts were familiar. I had thought them before.

But it did not feel like they originated with me.

Like my body no longer felt like it was mine. For two days I lay in my bed. Then, I got up and lay in the bath. I looked down at my body in the water. I lifted my arm. I lifted my leg. But there was no sense of connection. There was no sense that my limbs belonged to me.

I remember feeling surprised by this. I remembering thinking that was my body lying there in the water but I was elsewhere.

Where was elsewhere?

System: Disconnected

In the silence of the night
My mind began to unravel.

Something was released in me. It seemed to happen all at once, suddenly. Then I could not contain the thoughts, the words. They came to me, they poured out of me. And then they would not stop. In some kind of frenzied attempt to hold on to them I was trying to write them all down. This became an obsession, a tyranny. For a number of days, and nights, that then stretched into weeks, I did nothing but write down my thoughts, as they came to me. I had to write them down. I was terrified of losing them. To lose even one thought seemed a terrible thing. I was trying to hold on to my thoughts. I was trying to hold on to my self. I knew this. I felt my self to be precariously balanced. So long as I thought all the thoughts I was

Something rather than nothing.

But, throughout, I berated myself.

I wrote on the computer. Endlessly. And in notebooks.

For many months after I did not read what I had written during this time. Or even so much as glance inside the notebooks. When I look inside them now I see that there are long stretches where my handwriting is different. It scrawls on the page. The letters are more spaced out and the words less well formed. The long strokes look aggressive, edgy, pointy, in the way that they declare themselves. These long thick black strokes look like spiders' legs – unwieldy, and extending, unsightly, on the blankness of the page. And there are lots of dots. It seems like it was impossible for me to manage a full stop at this time. Completion was not something I could contemplate. It is disturbing to see such visual signs of my unbalanced state of mind.

The writing was a stream of consciousness. It was a stream of self-obliteration.

Like the body, the mind can only take so much tension. Like a rubber band... stretched... stretched... stretched... and in the end, it snaps...

I felt that I was on the edge.

What edge?

I was on the edge of my self, my world, and peering over...

And, it really is true... The nothingness... I never felt it... Quite like that before... It was everything I had ever feared...

This is what I am afraid of, I was thinking, and now I am going into it...

It was all in my body too... Feeling giddy, and shaking... Making so many mistakes as I typed the words... Having to keep typing... No longer knowing why I was typing... The wrong letters emerging... And every time, I had to go back over them... Like everything else...

I kept typing, but slower and slower...

So slow because I couldn't find the right keys... My fingers were heavy... Perhaps because it did not feel any longer like they were mine... It was like wading through the thickest darkest treacle... It required... such effort...

Yet ... I had to... continue... To find the words...

Then there was only lethargy... A heaviness... A flatness... Such a fatigue... Why did I keep going with it...?

I stopped

And the cord snapped...

Then it was like I went into the nothingness... And I stopped writing... It was like.....................

I stopped thinking...

Words didn't come to me...

Someone once told me that words are not so important, to hold on to... That they don't necessarily mean anything... But without words, I felt like I didn't have anything...

Left.

I felt nothing.

I realized nothing.
It was not an easy realization.

It wasn't like the blankness...

I fell into a void...

And there was truly nothing there…

How can I describe it?

Nothing defies description…

I can describe

Nothing

But…..

My fear

………..And just a sensation

Of emptiness

And

I was falling

    …. Falling

        … Falling…………..

And then I woke up, in the night, with my heart in my mouth –
as I have said.

I felt like a child.

I woke up to find that I was calling, silently...

Don't you know... You were supposed to rescue me...

In the story, the princess lies in the glass box, the prince comes and with a kiss, he wakes her up...

I want to wake up now... I don't want to be in the box any longer... How do you breathe in a glass box...? Didn't I tell you, that I am afraid of suffocation...? You know, you always said that you were...

There

But you do not hear me...

Don't you know, you are supposed to...

Rescue me, rescue me...

Wasn't I rescued before...?

And I am falling... falling... And I don't know where, or what, I am falling into... I am sure you were supposed to catch me...

Where are you? You told me that you were always there...

Now I really need you to be, and I do not ask, so easily...

I will not ask it, I will not ask it...

How do I know that you are still there...?

When it feels like everyone leaves me... Eventually... In one way or another...

I told you once, that my father didn't speak to me for two years... Later, he apologized... He said that he could not comprehend what he had been thinking...

You said that you were like my father: you meant the silences, I think, but I did not ask you to elucidate at the time, I just denied it.

I could not contemplate it.

Did I ever tell you that when I first saw you, I thought I recognized you. You seemed familiar. It was like I had always known you... Did I tell you this? I can't remember... Somehow it seems important to remember if I told you this...

Are you there?

You said that you were, before... In fact, it was you who pointed it out to me... You said to me that you were still there... And I still remember how you looked at me when you said it...

Once, I believe I told you how, when it feels like you are gone, That it feels like... You have dropped off the edge of the world...

In the middle of another night, I find myself thinking... What is mental distress... Is it a sickness? Am I sick? I feel sick, but this is not like any sickness that I have ever known...

Kierkegaard entitled one of his books, 'The Sickness Unto Death'. An audacious title. You could say that, as titles go, it is uncompromisingly bleak. Which is how people often think of his writing, but in fact, there is a lot of humour in it.

There is humour in all the blackness... This is generally recognized... Don't people talk of black humour...? Gallows humour...? In our long meetings at the hospital, when we go through all the deaths, and then we talk about the others who are dying, you wouldn't believe it but we laugh...

You would think, how can that be? But the laughter just emerges... And there is no disrespect in it. In fact, quite the opposite. It's like the laughter emerges out of caring... There is a lightness there... That touches on the blackness...

In fact, you could turn around the thought: I ask you, I challenge you, to imagine such meetings without laughter in them...

Black is never just black, there are many shades to blackness... There is even light within it...

There can be clarity in the darkest moments. You can even still think of others. There can be care there, within the blackness...

After the poet, Sylvia Plath, committed suicide, it was realized that before she gassed herself, she had not only taken the greatest care, to block off the gaps under the kitchen door with towels, so that the gas did not penetrate into the flat beyond, and harm her children, but she had also left them each a glass of milk and some bread, for when they awoke...

Until then, Plath had seen herself as Lady Lazarus: 'Dying is an art, like everything else. I do it exceptionally well...' Only that time, she did not come back... She did not intend to, she had made sure of that... Like the first time, when they dug her out, it seemed like a miracle that had led to her being found, and saved...

Maybe she had expected another miracle...

A miracle, or an intervention by Chance?

Plath was the golden girl. She did not reveal easily the blackness inside her. Except in her poetry. The blackness, and the lightness, the despair and the wry humour, together with her ferocious intelligence: it was all there in the poems.

At times, during these days, that stretched into weeks, I thought: have I gone to pieces...? And, if I have, how do I put myself back together?

Sometimes, when something gets broken, you can't fix it...

I thought about my mother and I wondered what she was thinking, when she put the pills to her lips and drove off to that lonely place and parked her car...

Afterwards, when I saw her, she was not... herself.

Later, she became very calm but strangely absent. Like she was no longer there. Which made me feel afraid.

When I was child, I wanted to see myself as like my mother. She cared for us children, always. She was always there, unlike my father. He was always writing, and he travelled around a lot. We scarcely saw him.

I tried to be caring, but I knew that I always put myself firmly in the centre of my world. I felt guilty about it, but then that's no good to anyone.

It's easy to feel guilty. Easier than doing what you sometimes know to be the right thing. Easier to do exactly what you want and then feel guilty afterwards... I remember joking about it with someone once, and saying that guilt was my middle name. He reminded me of it, on several occasions, when he thought that I was giving myself a hard time.

The attempt to be good was important to me, as a child you could say it was the project of my self. When my father castigated me for some misdemeanour, where I had been uncaring or selfish in a careless disregard for others, I experienced it with a fierce sense of shame which pierced me like an arrow and caused me to question my very right to exist.

I nearly didn't – exist, I mean – so I think I grew up feeling that somehow (someone?) had given me this life, but the question was, then, having been given it, what was I supposed to do with it?

I didn't know the answer to that question – I still don't – but somewhere along the way I knew that life was about care...

For care is an existential concept: it is our care that enables us to engage in the world and everyone and everything that we find within it. But this concept can be opened out: care has many forms.

So there I was in pieces... All these thoughts, bits of me... That didn't seem to fit together...

I thought: I have lost my mind. It felt like a very lucid thought. A very simple thought. Straightforward. And I thought it dispassionately. There was no feeling in it. And this thought was followed by another: If something is truly lost, can it ever be refound?

These words appeared in the form of a question, but there wasn't much wondering in it. Just a flatness. A deadness. They were just words, just eruptions of thoughts with no feeling in them.

But then I was also experiencing what you might call highs and lows...

Sometimes despair just tips over into exhilaration – like there is just nowhere left for it to go – but into a feeling of elation... And you just want to keep going with it, you are possessed by an all-consuming energy...

It happened first to me after the nothingness... I woke up in the night, in fact it was the early hours of the next morning... and something had shifted in me... And I just got up and started writing... But it was different this time... That was when the poems came to me... And it felt like such a wonderful feeling... I think because there was this heady rush of exhilaration and in the midst of it, suddenly, a steadiness of thought, a concentration, and poems just arose in this concentrated thinking, and for I while I found focus, it was like the poems centred me...

Such a strange delight...! I had never known such delight as this before...

Then I crashed again... Again into the flatness and the nothingness... That was a shock. But then I realized that it wasn't the same, because this time I knew that the nothingness had an end to it.... I was just waiting... And I am used to waiting...

When you crash... everything that was going so fast... just slows down... and comes to a gradual stop... the thoughts just wind down, it's like a battery going down... Less and less energy... the fatigue overwhelms you...

At first, after the nothingness, when the elation came, it had felt like it would last for ever... Such joy! For some days, I was writing round the clock from four in the morning until four in the afternoon... I barely ate... I did not think about my body at all... I was all mind... Or not so much mind... That would imply a place... for a coming together of thoughts, an integration... Whereas my thoughts flew out in all directions... They did not settle...

It was dizzying... It was like the film, *The Magic Roundabout*, which I watch with my son, where there is the scene when the roundabout starts to spin and it spins faster and faster, with all the children on it... And at first they are delighted... And then the delight slips away and you see their faces as they realize they are spinning away from the world...

They get trapped behind a layer of ice... Which seals them inside... They can only look out... and no one can reach them...

Therapists aren't supposed to lose their minds, I was thinking. But then therapists are people just like anyone else... We can't hold onto our selves at all times... In fact, in the past, there have been quite a few – some of the most famous and the most brilliant by all accounts – who went quite mad (not to put too fine a point on it)...

But nothing ever gets said – well, certainly not at the time... It's just not talked about...

I thought about a well-known therapist who recently killed herself... She was a leading figure in the psychotherapy world who had elicited great respect... Everyone was shocked, and saddened by it...

But I had heard that she did it responsibly... She had prepared the way... She finished with all her patients first... Is it possible to kill yourself in a responsible way...? I mean what about the people who are left behind?

We don't exist in isolation, everything we do has an impact on others... And I have seen some of those who have been left behind, and it is never easy...

It's easy to pretend we are individuals, with rights: a right to live one's own life... Or to extinguish it...

But do we have the right? What about the others? Do we have a right to extinguish their lives...? For does not death take many forms...?

Left behind, it can feel like you are dead... No longer in the world... Not really living.

Like the world has been deleted.

Many days had passed. I was lying in the bath. Looking down at my body, I was aware only of this strange feeling of disconnection.

I remember noting, dispassionately, at the same time, how my ribs now protruded.

I remember observing this, and thinking that I knew exactly what I was doing.

The bath was a space to think. Well, I was thinking everywhere, as I have said, I couldn't stop it. But the bath is a special place for me. I like the way it contains me. (My therapist once said it was like a womb for me – I objected, I thought that was a bit simplistic, but, on reflection, maybe she was right.) In the bath I feel contained, like I am in a box. I like that. In a box, but not enclosed.

Except my thoughts kept spilling out, unfortunately they were not contained... And I had to keep leaning over to write them down... And then the pages got wet...

I was lying in the bath, thinking, and then I became aware that there was somebody next door with a shovel... banging and scrapping... and I wanted to scream... (During those days, loud noises, or even soft ones had become unbearable to me...) I wanted to go out in the garden and scream at the person responsible for these noises that were grating... and scraping against my thoughts...

I almost thought about doing it. (This would have created quite a stir, for quite apart from my shouting, I would have been naked, but I don't think I would have cared about that.) It was a man. My next door neighbour had come out into the garden and I could hear them talking... I couldn't hear all the words... But they were talking about 'concrete' and 'foundations'... They were both laughing... I'm sorry to say that I wanted to kill them at that moment... Although I think, even then, I felt a little taken back at the violence of my reaction...

I was feeling angry...

And meanwhile, my cat was dashing round the place, up and down the hall, pulling the threads of the carpet, which he knows that I disapprove of... It was like my cat couldn't contain himself either... These mad bursts of energy... Followed by glances in my direction... Desperate for my attention...

I sat down at my computer... A baby crying in the street... Enough to drive you mad... If you weren't already...

Then a knock on the door... I ignored it... Then again... I went and answered it. It was the man who was working next door. He wanted to know if I had a manhole cover in the garden. I looked at him and tried to engage with the question... I could be normal... I thought I was putting on a good performance but he was looking at me strangely, so I explained that I wasn't 'well'. He was profusely apologetic. He was kind. Well, he had a kind face anyway. Then he went away and left me alone, as I wanted.

Towards the end of this period, I tried to go out. One day, the sun was shining. (It might have been on some of the other days, but I wouldn't have noticed, I had the curtains drawn.) Usually, I like the sun. When it's hot, it's close to an addiction for me; I have to get out there. But on this occasion, it felt like the sun was assaulting me. Like its rays were not just on my skin but penetrating me, burning me up inside. It was not pleasant. I scurried back into the house.

I began to feel confused about this urgent desire to record each and every thought. I felt out of control... I felt compelled... It had become a compulsion... I was possessed... It was like I was gripped by an external force...

Even at night, it would not leave me. I was in and out of bed, switching on the light, switching it off, scribbling the thoughts down as fast as they came to me... (But I persevered with getting back into bed, because I did not want to give way to 'it'...)

I was gripped by all these thoughts, all inter-linking and commenting on each other and then branching off into wild directions that then had to be pursued (each in a different notebook). In the course of a few weeks I completed eight notebooks, threw away countless pens (I found them some time later, at the bottom of my wastepaper basket) and my computer recorded ninety new documents, some of which went on for many pages...

When I was gripped it became imperative to write down all the different thoughts in the different journals and notebooks and if I couldn't find the particular notebook I wanted I felt like I couldn't tolerate the frustration and it felt like an impossible choice whether to let the thought go whilst I searched or whether I recorded it anywhere and then later I wouldn't know where to locate it or like with the typing did I keep going back over the words I was mistyping or did I continue at the risk of not being able to read it later for sometimes I was trying to type so fast every letter seemed wrong and then obviously in those instances I had to retype because otherwise the fear was that I would lose the thought... forever...

Yes, it would be lost for ever... The fear was about losing something for ever, that was it...

And then there was the awareness, all the while, on the fringes, that this desperate attempt to hold on to every thought was all connected to my anxiety about what was happening to me and my feeling that I was losing my mind, and I knew that each was amplifying the other: that I had the thought that I was losing my mind and then the anxiety that emerged out of that, which was a different anxiety to the first, and that the second anxiety just kept building and amplifying into some kind of force and then I was in a downward spiral... which I recognized from my work with patients.

The question was whether I could apply what I knew to my self. This was difficult because I was aware of a tension or, in fact, more of a head-on conflict, between a desire to come out of this way of thinking and an attraction, or fascination...

And I knew that this proliferation of thoughts, even the anxiety about them, was just a disguise, a cover-up for what lurked beneath... And I couldn't go into that... After the initial plummet, I could not return to that... These cascading thoughts kept me away, they protected me...

So I was telling myself that I had to let it run its course. That was my justification for letting myself go with it... But at the same time I was questioning myself as to whether I was giving way to an attraction that would prove to be somehow lastingly detrimental...

For once something is lost, can it ever truly be refound?

But then there was the pleasure in it – to feel the mind roaming so freely... To indulge in so many digressions...

To just let my mind go........

But where did it go? Question after question penetrated my consciousness...

And at times these never-ending questions persecuted me...

And the pervading sense of doubt heightened everything and gave me no tranquillity.

I was worrying and constantly fretting about letting my self go... And berating myself for not holding my self back... For not keeping a grip on my self... My self-watchfulness, an engrained habit from when I was a child, and essential to my work as a therapist, never left me. It infiltrated all the thinking, and, there was no doubt, made it all the more fatiguing.

But in truth, it did not feel a real choice... Perhaps maintaining the illusion that I was responsible, that I had chosen this, even though it made me feel guilty, concealed the degree of the compulsion which felt like it was overriding everything...

And I became aware that in losing my grip... Well, there was such a relief in it... I had not realized that I had been gripping on to my self so tightly for so long... What a relief to relinquish it...

Throughout, even though it was laced with anxiety, there was a heady exhilaration in all this thinking, and somehow, when I was in it, I lost sight of how it ebbed and flowed and how at some later point, this mad delight would then would tip over into fatigue... irritation... anxiety...

The mania was exciting but exhausting... It could only hold me for so long...

Then came the fatigue and I fell back into the flat despair... Emptiness... Desolation...

And then outside reality intervened. My son returned from being on holiday with his father and I had to refind my usual self for a few hours a day. I found that I could do this. Although I had to psyche myself up for it and go through lengthy mental preparations, I found that, towards the appointed time each day when I needed to collect my son, something strange seemed to happen. The thoughts began to pick themselves up and withdraw away from me... I could find my steady space with him and for those few hours I could re-enter his world... It was not so difficult. Although I was aware of a tension... of waiting... until I could let them reappear. And, later, after he went to bed, the thoughts came again thick and fast, and gave me no peace and there was scarcely any exhilaration in it, there were just too many...

But it had to run its course...

When I went to pick up my son after his return from holiday, he had leaped into my arms and hugged me, and I had cried, although I don't think he saw since his face was over my shoulder.

We took the stairs rather than the lift, as we usually did. He was excited, animated, telling me everything, and as we did this he was bouncing a little ball as we descended and exclaiming at where it landed each time. He liked how, since it was so small and so bouncy, it could veer off into so many different directions and just keep going... It hit the walls, the ceiling, and down the stairs again. We both watched it. We were marvelling at its speed, how it could reach so many different landing points and we were laughing. However, I could not resist warning him, feebly, of the possibilities of its disappearance into some obscure corner of the stairwell. 'You don't want to lose it,' I said.

But my son was not concerned. He continued regardless. I don't think he even heard me, as he was too busy gleefully pursuing the ball as it rolled down the stairs.

*

A month almost to the day after I had first heard of my patient's death, I went for a walk down to the local shops, and it felt like time had slipped into another season.

Walking across the park, there was an autumnal chill to the air and the wind was chasing the leaves so that they scooped and whirled, in a frenzied dance. The trees were shedding their leaves fast. It seemed that autumn was to take place in a day this year. The noise of the wind in the leaves was less of a rustling, and more of a roar. Its fury frightened me.

I was feeling delicate. Not fully there. It felt like everything around me had more of a claim to exist than me and that all the trees, the leaves, the grass, the houses, all were proclaiming this to me in the loud solidity of their presence.

By contrast, I felt small and fragile: almost non-existent.

But I hastened on and tried to think about other things.

And a week later, I went back to work.

PART IV

'Where flames a word to witness for us both?
You – wholly real. I – wholly mad.'

Paul Celan

After

My writings were none of them finished; new thoughts intruded ever, extraordinary, inexcludable associations of ideas bearing infinity for term. I cannot prevent my thought's hatred of finish; about a single thing ten thousand thoughts, and ten thousand inter-associations of these ten thousand thoughts arise, and I have no will to eliminate or to arrest these, nor to gather them into one central thought, where their unimportant but associated details may be lost.

Fernando Pessoa

There is a paradox within reflection: it offers a pathway to finding oneself, yet, one can also lose oneself in its myriad twists and turns. Caught up in our perplexity, we can find ourselves wandering in an endless labyrinth that tantalizes and confounds us with hidden depths and secrets which will never be revealed.

When, I contemplated what I had experienced, it seemed to me that the highs and the lows to which I had felt myself subjected, epitomized the heady excitement of hyper-reflexivity, a state of mind that knows no calm. I remembered how Kafka had once written in his diary of the 'wild tempo' of 'an introspection [that] will suffer no idea to sink tranquilly to rest but must pursue each one into consciousness, only itself to become an idea, in turn to be pursued by renewed introspection'.

I realized, also, that this excitement in thinking was not altogether foreign to me. And I recognized this almost feverish state of mind from certain times when I had seen and heard my father talk when he was immersed in his writing.

I had also heard him talk about his father. The mind is a delicate thing, under extreme external pressures it can become unhinged. In my grandfather's case, like for many men of his generation, it was the Great War. Possibly, he had a predisposition, but it was the War that tipped him over the edge. At the age of nineteen, he had seen his best friend killed in action. He was the only survivor of all his friends who fought alongside him. Can any mind survive such horrors intact? In his case, he was on medication for the rest of his life. Every once in a while the traumas he had witnessed would break through his normally cheery disposition and he would become paranoid: fearful and inspiring fear, too. My father told of how on one occasion he carried an axe with him to the doctor's – 'for protection'. As children, he and his brother learnt to be watchful for the signs just before their father would tip over into one of his states. He would go onto a 'high' and become very excited and then he would tip over into paranoia or he would lose his memory, and any sense of who he was. Several times he went missing for some days, and was eventually brought home by the police.

I knew my grandfather only briefly. He died when I was very young. I remember how he used to take me for walks in the woods and show me all the red squirrels. One image remains of him pointing up into the trees. It was probably a squirrel, but what I remember is his face as he turned towards me and the way the light slanted through the trees and fell upon the leaves …

*

In his book, *Into the Silent Land*, the neuropsychologist, Paul Brok writes, 'Anyone who has worked with patients on acute hospital wards will tell you that you cannot resonate with every tremor of feeling, and that sometimes there are visions of horror and raw fear that can only be observed obliquely...' In such circumstances, 'perfect, constant empathy would be suicidal,' he comments.

However, Brok is a neuropsychologist, he works within the medical model, his primary focus is on the physical, the organic interworkings of the brain, and how they inform the mind. The psychotherapist is, by definition, up close; the mind with all its feeling, its fears, its visions of horrors, both actual and perceived, is the subject. It is difficult therefore for the psychotherapist to 'observe obliquely'.

For the psychotherapist, it is perhaps more a case of being able to move up close, and then to move away again, to relocate oneself, mentally, once one has left the patient. This skill is developed in training, one learns how to engage and then to disengage. This is not always easy, you can lose your balance for a while; however, the most important thing is that it is not to the detriment of the patient. The patient may feel that she is falling apart, you have to stay firm, you have to hold your self together, as a firm base for the patient. There may be times, when you might fall apart afterwards, for a while, the endeavour then is simply for you to put yourself back together.

This requires concentration, focus, insight and a strong will.

On this occasion, I had not managed it.

And one thing had led to another.

*

It seemed to me, initially, when I first began to consider it, that my experience reflected the tyranny of thinking.

But then I had to remind myself that the thinking, and the thoughts were not some abstract force that descended upon me, although it had felt that way. No, they emanated from me. And if I experienced them as persecutory, which at times I did, that was me persecuting myself.

It was me who took my self apart. I felt guilt about that. Layer upon layer of guilt revealed itself, snaking one between the another.

I felt guilt that I had lost it. Lost what? Lost the plot, my mind, my self...?

I had pulled myself to bits.

But why did I take my self apart?

Guilt again reared its head and stared me in the face.

Throughout, there had been the repeated question, which, cruelly, kept resurfacing:

Why her, and not me...?

It was not so much a cognition. More a feeling. There had been many overlaps between myself and my patient. I had experienced a close identification. I had known this.

And then?

When she died:

'It could have been me – it should have been me…'

Such thoughts were not unfamiliar to me. I was feeling what is known as survivor guilt. The guilty sense of responsibility of the one who survives. Yet knowing this didn't seem to help much. In fact, the reasoning made no difference to me…

Because I couldn't reason myself out of the feeling…

And the knowing: for I had known her fears, that had reared up at her in the nights, when they could no longer be bolted in. And I did not know if these fears had evaporated, after she had brought them out and tentatively entrusted them to me.

I realized fully now, what I had half-realized at the time, what I had realized then only obliquely: that I had been caught, at some level, in magical thinking. Yes, I had wanted to rescue my patient – from her fears, from death itself…? (And, in so doing, to rescue myself too?)

I realized that to some extent I had entered into her fantasy: she would not die. (Nor would I.)

And when I discovered the news of her death I felt shock, and I felt that I had failed. It felt like I had abandoned her. She had died and I wasn't there… I was on holiday.

Perhaps, in all my thinking, I had been trying to obliterate myself, to punish myself...

And to see if I could survive?

*

My patient and I were close in age. I knew that there were many overlaps between her life and mine. Yet, in my mind, somewhere, something had got confused, or there was some overlap that I was struggling to comprehend...

When I was very young, my mother had a miscarriage... In my mind, as a child, that baby was always the sister that I never had...

And I remember thinking to myself: 'Why did she die, and why not me?'

After all, I knew that I should have died.

That I nearly died when I was born.

For, they told my father

I would not
be

born.

Through my life I have struggled to understand this. As a child, I felt that I was not supposed to be...

How can you comprehend a life that nearly wasn't a life at all?

How do you comprehend that being is a breath away from nothingness?

*

Later, I thought about her family, and how she would have died with them all around her. I knew that they were closely-knit, that they would have been there.

As time passed, I thought more about them. Later, I tried to phone, and then I sent a letter, but there was no response.

I think I tried to make contact both for them and for me. I wanted to know that she hadn't been alone.

*

It was in this period that one morning I woke up, with the strangest dream image. It was that of a toad, swallowing a crystal. Co-existing with the image were these words in my head: 'The toad swallowed the crystal and choked on it.'

The predominant feeling as I awoke was one of sadness and loss.

I have many thoughts and associations that connect from the dream which do not take me to one place and one interpretation.

What did seem clear to me, however, was that something bad or ugly attempted to swallow something beautiful, yet the crystal was so hard and so durable that it could not be swallowed, so it survived.

I had the feeling that the toad died.

****

That day at the station when you would not speak to me... I think I told you, later, how it was as if, suddenly, within a moment, I lost all sense of who I was... What I was doing... Where I was going... Everything went blank... It was like suddenly a void opened up in me...

That was the first time...

Since I was a child...

After I got off the train, that was the first time that I saw Dr O.

It is strange. I have no memory of it, there is only a blankness. Yet I must have walked there. It is close to the station in any case.

I remember that Dr O was very patient with me. At first, I could not speak. The words just would not come to me. I remember only a space that just kept opening up, and a sensation, like I was falling... And all the while, his words just echoed in my head, like empty sounds, since I was unable to connect myself up to them.

Dr O told me I was clearly suffering a traumatic reaction. In the hours that followed, he gave me first 5ml of D. I had not taken tranquillizers since I was a child but I noted no effect. A half hour later, he gave me another 5ml. Still nothing. Dr O continued to increase the dose and monitor my reaction. I was sitting in an empty room. I remember sitting in a chair and looking at the wall. I do not remember thinking anything. The whole day passed in this way. In the late afternoon he encouraged me to stay, at least for that night, but I remember by then I was adamant about leaving. I was calmer. It was like the pain had all been blanked out. In the blankness, strangely, then, I could find some words. Some scattered thoughts. I had somewhere to go to, I told him, I had someone who would look after me. He was kind: he ordered me a taxi and put me in it, he prescribed 40ml of D for the next few days and told me to come back and see him at the end of the week.

I went back to see him twice more. That was in January. In the month that I was off work that August, I thought about going back to see Dr O. But, instead, I went to see my GP. I don't remember much of what she said, so much as her soft manner, which made me weep, and that, having established that I posed no risk to myself, she told me that it was clear to her that I was suffering an intense grief reaction, and at the end of that first week, she signed me off for three further weeks to recover.

*

The Impossible

There were
Possibilities

Yet it is

The Impossible

Stretching before me
Clothed

In silence

No sound
In the dark

Impossible

Yet
To imagine

The silence

Dropped
Abandoned

To live

Still

Impossible

Dream

Lost

In night's shroud

A star's light
Once was

There

Blinking
In the darkness.

*

'Unhappy that I am, I cannot heave
My heart into my mouth'

*

I told you how you amazed me…

You asked me why, and I could not answer you.

I could never explain, and I sensed that you wanted to know,
That for you, the explanation was all.

I thought that I had spoken to you about everything,
But for you, it was
nothing

And, yes, I know, in the beginning, I was the one who had said,
'It's all or nothing…'

Then I realized my mistake, did I not admit it?

*

You know, you told me once, that I was different to you. That was the last time I saw you.

There seemed, to me, to be a sadness in your voice when you said that.

Did that mean that you thought that we had to be, in some way, the same...?

Once, a long time before, you had told me that you thought we were too much the same...

Afterwards, I wondered about this...

Two statements that contradict seem to cancel each other out.

Nothing
Then remains

Just impossibility.

*

In life, there is contradiction, and then there is paradox. In contradiction one thing cancels out the other.

In paradox, two things that seemingly contradict, can co-exist...

Like:

I told you everything and I told you nothing

Or

You told me nothing and you told me everything.

Paradoxically, two people can be different, and the same: both co-existing. Can they not?

*

Do you remember that time we were walking down the street? I was pursuing you with words, when you didn't want to hear them.

I suddenly stopped, right there on the pavement, defeated, exasperated, both with myself and with you.

'Oh, why do I persist?' I said.

I said it flatly, it was hardly even a question.

But you turned round to face me and responded.

'Because you know that I am unhappy,' you said.

I still remember these words and the expression on your face when you said them...

*

You were right (weren't you, always?) when you said, words are not real. You were right in one way perhaps: words do not make up the whole of reality.

Tell me, what was more real – the words that you said to me, or the way you looked at me when you said them?

*

My son sometimes asks me to tell him what is real and what is a dream. He asks me if he is dreaming now…

'How can I know,' he says, 'that this isn't all a dream?'

I try to reassure him that it isn't. It is true and real, and I am standing before him… Sometimes I try to make a joke about it.

'Pinch me, so I know,' he says. I do so… 'Harder,' he says. I say that I do not want to hurt him. 'I need to know for sure,' he says.

Can you be dreaming, and not know it?

*

I walk into a room. All is as it was. In my dream, the room is very familiar to me. She is standing next to the window and turns towards me as I come through the door. We look at each other. I am thinking, 'You are not real. You are dead. I have conjured you up. I have conjured you up from my imagination.'

She approaches me. I am prepared for her to suddenly fade away, like a spectre, to become at one with the air around us. I am rooted to the spot. Until she stands in front of me.

Then I clasp her, like I did that day when we said goodbye. I did not know then that it would be the last time. I remember noticing the feel of her skin and how fleshy her arms were. In the dream, again, to my surprise, I feel the warmth of her flesh, and my heart lifts, an overwhelming relief floods over me, and I am weeping, and she says: 'I know.'

Then I wake up.

My dream is telling me, what I know already. I cannot grasp it. I cannot grasp that she is dead, just like I cannot grasp that my patient, Mina, is dead...

She died. Mina died. They both died in the same week...

Yet, I should be able to grasp this simple fact and accept it.

Why can't I?

Always the question, spoken or unspoken:

How can it be...? How can anything be, and then not be?

..............Death is just incomprehensible to me.............

And then: '...But I should be able to grasp it... To comprehend it...'

Then round again,
And always ending with the same thought:

>   *'It cannot be...'*

'And we are all going to die...O pinewoods gloomy at dusk.....'

Everything in me rebels in the face of death... Non-being...Theirs and my own...

*

'I know,' she says.   In my dream, she reassures me.

In my dream, I know she understands. She can see the relief in my eyes.

In my dream she is just as she was in life: a reassuring presence.

I was aware of this, when she was alive and how she was solicitous towards me, motherly, although the gap in our ages was not so great.

I was aware of this, but I did not reflect on it.

Undoubtedly, we do not always reflect on the relationships that we have.   There are those that we take for granted. The relationship happens in passing, in the midst of things, barely noted for itself.   It can be that it is not until someone is gone that you realize the connection.   You realize once it is broken.

****

Once, I dreamt of you.

We were in that city, where we never went.

Not together.

In my dream I arrived there and I knew that you were there, too.

Then, suddenly, I caught a brief glimpse of you in the distance, across the water. You were crossing a bridge, and heading in the opposite direction to me. I went to shout, but no sound came.

But I knew that you wouldn't have heard me, you were too far away, and, besides, you did not know I was there.

Once, later, I thought I heard you calling...

I remember, I was just leaving... I was boarding the boat.

I hesitated and looked back, but the wind blew my hair into my face. And I saw nothing.

The White of the Eye

'Night is also a sun'
Zarathustra

Glistening pearl
Within

The darkness
Of the sea bed

Pearl
Of
Whiteness

Such brightness
And deadness

It does not seem possible

That those could be pearls
That were his eyes

No dark within them
No seeing

White
Light

White of the eye
Unseeing

Oh God,
Give me the night

Of your blind man's eyes
Give me the dark night
For I do not want to see

The bright light
Hurts
My eyes

Such bright white light.

And then
In the garden
The night

Fell

So suddenly
It fell

The breeze
Was slight

And the leaves
Sighed

Do not leave
Me

No words
On my lips

Only the silence

And your breath
On my cheek

Before the light flickered
And the night fell
Around me

And I did not know
I could not know

That the night
Would be
So dark

That the light
Would be
So long

Coming -
But it came

With a gentle stirring
Of the leaves

A gentle stirring
Of the breeze

The light came

And I breathed
Again

Slowly

I opened my eyes
White eyes
And dark within

White
Within
The night

All seeing.

*

Bright

White

Light

Everything was white.

In my dream I stepped into my garden and, suddenly, I was surrounded by large white flowers, all around me.

Pure white. Like a curtain of whiteness...

And so bright: I could never have imagined such brightness...

I felt wonder.

I turned and, suddenly, you were standing there, beside me. I said to you: 'La Dame aux Camélias...'

Fragile whiteness.

You said: 'Wings of Desire...'

And I saw a fleecy, feathery whiteness. Experienced the sensation of all-encompassing softness. Velvety whiteness. Like a physical presence, to be touched, and felt, yet not of this world. An ephemeral whiteness. I was thinking of white flowers, of a woman who dies... Yet you referred me to the wings of angels.

*

I entered a room and I saw three white forms. Each was placed equidistant from the other inside their glass box. Each was perfectly rounded. Fashioned from white marble, they appeared so smooth, so solid.

A beauty of colour and of form
in their whiteness.

So solid
And contained

In their glass box.

White beauty.
And white perfection.

*

When I was a child, I used to imagine that I was inside a glass box.

I once saw a picture of Sleeping Beauty. It was in a storybook. She was lying in her glass box, and I remember that she was smiling as she slept...

I imagined that she was dreaming many dreams.

Perhaps, for me, the glass box functioned as a boundary. Between myself and the world. I imagined that when I woke up, I would be able to see out. But not be reached.

I guess I felt safe, in my box.

Safe and protected.

So what was I protecting myself from? What, for me, did the world represent?

And did Sleeping Beauty want to be woken up?

For, if the prince had not come, would Sleeping Beauty not have continued to sleep and dream for all eternity...?

*

I still remember you.
Should I not? Would you prefer that I didn't?

You know, the other day I was walking along the road. It was early in the morning and I saw a young woman coming towards me, dressed in a suit. Then I looked down and saw she was carrying a pint of milk, and upon her feet were a pair of fluffy pink slippers. I smiled, because I thought of the kind of witty remark you might have made, had you been walking with me.

You know, before I met you, I am not sure that I would have even noticed. So, you see, you showed me how to look at the world differently...

Or even to look at the world, when sometimes I forget...

Sometimes I forget to notice things...

Let alone, laugh about them...

Maybe, before, I didn't choose to notice them, because I never realized that it was possible to laugh so much...

It seems important that I tell you this.

You may not think so... For it is true that these are simply words that I am speaking to you...

Yet (and surely, you cannot deny it?) is it not also true that within your words were your thoughts, and feelings, about people, about things...

About me?

In this way, I can say

That your words

were

everything:

to me.

*

I remember the night that I dreamed of whiteness.

So many flowers before me, all around me...

Like a white curtain, they appeared and I stood there, just looking. I drank in the sight of them. I was just... in wonder at them.

Everything was whiteness and lightness...

It was then, as I gazed, that I realized that you were there, beside me. I did not need to turn and look at you, it was enough that you were there. I spoke to you, and you replied. I saw flowers and I thought of white camellias. I thought of a woman, dying. You thought of angels. In the film, you named, the angels are human presences: they seem to belong to the earth. I remembered then how the wings of the angels had filled the screen: all that whiteness in the darkness. So white, so feathery, and fleecy...

They had a physicality, an earthly pragmatism, and yet they were ephemeral too...

The wings of the angels bore them aloft...

We knew that the angels were not really of this earth: we knew that they resided elsewhere... Although it could not be known, where they resided...

*

I was looking at an art work. There was a square with a cube within it. The cube was a raised block positioned at the end of an empty line.

I was gazing at the empty line in the painting.

The artist traced his finger along the line and finished up at the cube. He explained how the cube was made from the material that had been gathered up, which had then left the empty line.

'It is like when you walk through snow and push it with your feet,' he said. 'You can go from there and end up here.' I could see now that it was a connecting line. Like a trail.

'You see,' he said, 'something gets taken away, yet something else is created.'

*

A woman was telling me how many years before she had been coming out of an anaesthetic for a major operation, when she had, what she called, an 'uncanny' experience.

She described the strangest sensation... She said that she had experienced this white light. That there had been nothing but white light. Then, as she was telling me this, she corrected herself and said, that, in fact, it hadn't been so much a white light, more just a whiteness or a nothingness. 'I know this makes no sense,' she said, and, pausing she looked at me. Then she continued, 'It was the strangest thing,' she said, 'but it was just like nothing all around me. Only,' she added, 'there was no 'me', 'it was like I was just a feeling...'

And it was just incredible, she said, the feeling of joy, such that she could not really describe...

Then, suddenly, she had become aware that someone was patting her hand vigorously, and calling her by her Christian name. It was the surgeon. It took her a moment to realize as she came to, since he had never called her by her Christian name before...

And as she opened her eyes, she told him wonderful she felt, such that she had not wanted to come back...

A few days later, one of the nurses had commented how they had 'nearly lost her in there'. The nurse said that, technically speaking, she had died for a few moments.

It was just the strangest thing, this woman told me.

She also told me that dying held no fear for her now...

*

The man sitting before me told me how he used to go deep-sea diving.

He described how as you descend deeper and deeper the colours change. First as you are submerged and descend there is the red, then there is the blue, the green and, finally, there is the black.

Deep down in the furthest depths of the sea you can see only pitch blackness.

Then, he told me, you switch on your torch. And the colours hit you.

Deep down in the sea, there are such colours there, you cannot imagine, he said.

At that moment, when you switch on your torch it is as if all the colours leap out at you... There is so much life down there, he said, that for a moment it takes your breath away...

All the colours... They are so much more than you, he said. But they can become part of you, they are with me now, as I remember them...

Once you have seen such a thing, you never forget it...

I don't have to dive now to see them, he said. All those colours deep down in the blackness...

Before

'But this: to hold
death, the whole of death, so gently,
even before life's begun and not be mad
– that's beyond description!'

Rainer Maria Rilke, *Fourth Duino Elegy*

Sometimes, a strong fear of death can be related to one's birth. Whether some body memory of a birth trauma is retained, or, whether, on some level and from an early age, the knowledge of a difficult birth is imbibed, the end result is the same: the child has a sense of his or her existence as precarious. This can also happen with children who become seriously ill, or who have a childhood brush with death in some way or another. Somehow, as you grow up you never feel that you can take your being alive for granted.

The thought that you nearly died can haunt you. It is like your shadow, it is always there.

What might have been, and what will be, is always there.

The psychoanalyst, R D Laing, termed it ontological insecurity. It is not necessarily a fear of death as such, but a fear of non-being.

'I nearly died when I was born,' I remember telling my friends in the school playground. I was around five or six years old. No doubt, I wanted to gain their attention and to impress them.

The story of my birth had been told to me for as long as I could remember, by my parents. I knew everything: how the umbilical cord had been knotted, and how my father had been told that whilst they could save my mother, I would be born dead. How, against all the odds, miraculously, the surgeon was able to save me. And how, apparently, he had displayed the knotted cord, in a glass jar, ever after as an inspiration for his students.

In my parents' narrative, it was the surgeon who was the hero. But, in my telling, I was the centre of the story: 'I was going to be born dead!' (I had a feel for the dramatic.) Yet, I had survived, I told my friends. In my account, the focus was on my life and death struggle that I had won. My birth was my achievement. After all, it was I, who on the very threshold of life, had come up against death and conquered it. And, clearly, if you can conquer death, you can conquer anything...

Yet, beneath the bravado, on the fringes of my consciousness, the flip side to the fantasies of omnipotence was an acute awareness of my own fragility. My mortality loomed large. Together with a vague terror at the thought that I could not have been. 'I nearly died when I was born.' From the beginning, my death was there at the forefront of my existence.

I knew that I had been saved, but by who? By myself? By the surgeon? By God?

As a child, I liked to think that I had been saved because it made me feel important. But then, on the heels of that thought came the questions: why? And could I not have been? These questions permeated my consciousness.

From when I was very young, I didn't sleep well at nights. I had nightmares from which I woke up screaming. My mother told me how once, how when I was around two years old, my father had to be called out of a lecture he was giving to come home and placate me. Apparently, he was the only one who could calm me.

I remember how, from when I was a young child, in my dreams it was like I had fallen off the edge of the world. I was always in darkness and falling through infinity. Falling without end. From an early age, I remember visualizing the darkness of the universe that opened out before you and went on forever. It terrified me.

In my dreams I was lost in the darkness and when I awoke the world that I awoke to seemed unreal to me. How did I know I wasn't still dreaming? At times life seemed like the dream, a brief dream, locked within time – and the reality? It was infinity, that yawning black chasm.

It was only years later that I read of a similar fear of non-being in Nabokov's memoir, *Speak Memory*. And felt a stab of recognition. For, in the awesome perfection of his prose, Nabokov's description encapsulated my own experience perfectly. Nabokov writes that 'the cradle rocks above an abyss, and common sense tells us that our existence is but a brief crack between two eternities of darkness'. He describes his feeling of panic when, as a child, he saw a home movie taken a few weeks before his birth and in it, caught a glimpse of an empty pram. It had 'the smug encroaching air of a coffin...' as if, 'in the reverse course of events, his very bones had disintegrated.'

For Nabokov, the empty pram clearly denotes his absence, that he was not there, but not only before his birth, for equally and ominously it signals his future absence: his future non-being.

Nabokov describes how this terrible realization fuelled a revolt within him that has outlived his childhood: 'Nature,'' he writes 'expects a full-grown man to accept the two black voids, fore and aft, as stolidly as he accepts the extraordinary visions in between... I rebel against this state of affairs. I feel the urge to take my rebellion outside and picket nature.'

I remember well, as a child, trying to comprehend a world that did not have me in it. And the fear of not having existed before my birth was just as vivid as my fear about what would happen to me after my death. (The irrational question: Where was I, before I was born? lingered a great deal round the edges of my consciousness.) In fact, out of the two, my fear about my pre-existence, and that I was nearly not born at all, probably evoked the most anxiety, perhaps because, as a child, it was closer to me than death was, then. Whilst I never took my living for granted, death seemed potentially a long way off to me, just as my birth is now.

So it has reversed. And as I grow older it is more of my future non-being that I am thinking...

After...

You sent me
One last text

One word –

And a full stop

After

I remembered
It was you

Who once remarked, wryly
How we could never

Stop

Apologizing

After

More time passed

I was moving house,
As I packed up my things
I came across a book:

Opening the flyleaf

Your name
Leapt
Out.

I do not recall now
The book's full title

I see
      only
           one
                word

Remembering

upon its front cover

It was
an analysis
of memory:

             how it forms

                     and de-forms

us

from the beginning

we are

      Nothing

But

Our memories

          leaving

their imprint

          upon

               us:

upon the mind

Only, in the beginning
it is more

the body

remembering

I sent it back to you
Along with a note
Inviting you to meet
Like we used to do

Recalling you

Before
Your silence

On the edge
of the world

Memory and desire

stirring

Calling
In the silence

And recalling

Words unspoken

Memories flying away from me
Like butterfly wings

Touching my face

Before

Their shadow descends
Their wings beating

Words of no speech

Outside appearance

Nothing

But night

And a thousand stars
Behind my eyelids

Hearing a gasp
Like the world

Disappearing

But maybe
It was you

And me

Falling

After

Postscript

'And the end and the beginning were always there
Before the beginning and after the end.'

It was autumn. In the woods the sun was still bright, as it slanted through the leaves and hit the paths at our feet. I was out walking with my son. We stopped on an old iron bridge and looked down onto the disused railway track beneath, now grassed over, and tightly embraced on either side by thick bushes and trees. We looked down from the bridge, into the space where, all around us, the leaves were changing and falling. I blinked in the brightness, and I saw flashes of yellow, glinting and floating all around us. For a second, the distant voices of other walkers seemed to ebb away and there was a momentary silence. And everything in the wood was still. For a second, I experienced the strangest feeling, as if there was only us, myself and my son, in the world, together with the floating leaves, falling.

The words flashed into my head. All is always now.

Then I looked at my son's face and saw that he was laughing.

In remembrance of my father
who died on 7 April 2008:

'in a shroud of roses
an incandescent teardrop
proclaims the day'

Georges Bataille

'Do you realize
That everyone you know
Some day
Will die?'

Lyric by The Flaming Lips

Notes

Reference is made to the following authors and works:

iv *'And if the earthly has forgotten you...'*, Rainer Maria Rilke, from 'The Sonnets to Orpheus: Second Series', verse 29, *Duino Elegies and the Sonnets to Orpheus*, tr. A. Poulin, Jr (New York: Mariner Books, 2005), p.195.

vii *'The night is my nudity...'* Georges Bataille, from 'Oresteia', *The Impossible*, tr. R. Hurley (San Francisco: City Lights Books, 1991), p.147.

25 *'ineluctable modality of the visible...'* and p. *'signatures of all things'*, from James Joyce, *Ulysses* (Cambridge: Oxford University Press, 1983), p.47. I am indebted to Mark Rosenthal's linking of Joseph Beuys' vitrines with his interest in James Joyce, in Mark Rosenthal, *Joseph Beuys, Actions, Vitrines, Environments* (Menil Collection: Houston).

34 *'I rise with my long red hair...'* : The actual lines from Sylvia Plath's 'Lady Lazarus' are as follows: 'Out of the ash/I rise with my red hair/And I eat men like air.' From *Collected Poems*, ed. Ted Hughes (London: Faber & Faber, 1981).

36 *'The lips of your night...'* lines from 'Maithuna', *The Collected Poems of Octavio Paz*, ed. and tr. Eliot Weinberger (New York: New Directions Books, 1987).

46 *'We are nothing, neither you nor I...'* from Georges Bataille, *Inner Experience*, ed. and tr. Leslie Anne Boldt (New York: State University of New York Press, 1988), p. 94.

57 *'The leap of the wave...'* lines from 'Youth', *Collected Poems of Octavio Paz, 1987*, p.255.

69 *'Between the essence'*, T.S.Eliot, 'The Hollow Men' from *Collected Poems 1909-1962*, (London: Faber & Faber, 1963), p.92.

75 *'And the night'*, Rilke, 'The First Elegy', *Duino Elegies and the Sonnets to Orpheus*, p.5.

75 *'I ask you to follow me...'* Bataille, *Inner Experience*, p. 198.

81 *'On Margate Sands'*, T.S. Eliot, 'The Fire Sermon' in 'The Waste Land', *Collected Poems*, p.74.

119 *'Where flames a word'*, Paul Celan, 'I know you', *Selected Poems and Prose of Paul Celan*, tr. John Felstiner (New York: Norton, 2001), p.245.

123 *'My writings were none of them finished'* Fernando Pessoa, *A Centenary Pessoa*, ed. E. Lisboa & L.C. Taylor (Manchester: Carcanet Books, 1995), p.203.

123 *'wild tempo'*, Kafka's diary, 16 January 1922 quoted in A. Heidsieck, 'Kafka's narrative ontology', *Philosophy and Literature*, 11, 1987, 250.

124 *'Anyone who has worked with patients on acute hospital wards'* Paul Broks, *Into the Silent Land*, (London: Atlantic Books, 2003), p. 59.

135 *'Unhappy that I am,'* These words are spoken by Cordelia, in William Shakespeare's *King Lear*, Act I. Sc I, lines 93-94.

141 *'And we are all going to die...'* from the poem 'Triumphal Ode', Pessoa, *Centenary Pessoa*, 1995, p.88.

159 'But this: to hold/Death,' Rilke, 'The Fourth Elegy', *Duino Elegies and The Sonnets to Orpheus*, p.31.

163 'the cradle rocks above an abyss' and 'Nature expects a full-grown man' Vladimir Nabokov, *Speak Memory: An Autobiography Revisited* (London: Penguin Books, 1969), p.17.

170 *Memory and desire stirring*, T.S. Eliot, 'The Burial of the Dead', in 'The Waste Land', *Collected Poems*, p.63.

173 'And the end and the beginning' T.S.Eliot, 'Burnt Norton', from 'Four Quartets', *Collected Poems*, p. 194.

177 'in a shroud of roses', Georges Bataille, *Guilty*, tr. Bruce Boone (Venice CA: The Lapis Press, 1988), p.73.

As an existential psychotherapist, my thinking and my clinical work is imbued with the writings of Martin Heidegger whose lifelong project was no less than to seek to comprehend Being. Heidegger's starting point was to question the common preconception of 'a self' that exists in isolation. In his seminal work *Being and Time*, published in 1925, he challenged the subject /object divide that had underpinned Western philosophy since Descartes and explored how humans always come into being in a context, as being-in-the-world: that we always exist only in our relationships to our world and the people we find within it.

My text owes much to Heidegger's later work, in which he continued to develop a wider understanding of Being, as that which exists beyond us, whilst also incorporating us. In particular, the influences upon this text are *What is Called Thinking?* (1954) in which Heidegger examines thinking as 'the house of Being' and also his *Pathmarks* (1967), a collection of essays and lectures, spanning 1919-1961, including 'What is

Metaphysics?' and 'Introduction to "What is Metaphysics" ' in which he examines the Nothing within Being.

But finally, this book would not have been as it is without my reading of Georges Bataille, who (following Nietzsche) believed in going beyond knowledge, and suffering, towards passion, joy, ecstasy, the rupture of all 'possible', embracing one's inner experience – yet always in consciousness of others, that ultimately, we find ourselves in communication.

Acknowledgements

I wish to express my appreciation to all those have helped me. Most particularly, to Luci Moja Strasser, for her wisdom and constructive encouragement over many years; Amanda Lipman, who embarked on the existential path with me from the beginning, and who has been my touchstone ever since; and Kathy Briscoe, whose constancy and support I cherish, together with her thoughtful enthusiasm. Thanks go to Blake Morrison and Darian Leader, for reading and commenting on early drafts of this book, and encouraging me through difficult times. Also, to John Burnside, whose penetrating comments propelled me onwards. I am grateful to Elizabeth Boyd, Cristina Harnagea Sheppard and Janet Seller, who all read my final version and offered warm and generous feedback. My heartfelt thanks go to my publisher, John Hunt, for his faith in my text.

I owe much to Laurence O'Toole, whose broad intellect, wit and insight has contributed so much to my thinking; together we brought about and shared those unforgettable moments of pain and joy on the night of 1 December 1999. My son Frank has made his mark upon this book, his thoughts and questions have inspired me and his zest for life is second to none.

BOOKS

O is a symbol of the world, of oneness and unity. In different cultures it also means the "eye," symbolizing knowledge and insight. We aim to publish books that are accessible, constructive and that challenge accepted opinion, both that of academia and the "moral majority."

Our books are available in all good English language bookstores worldwide. If you don't see the book on the shelves ask the bookstore to order it for you, quoting the ISBN number and title. Alternatively you can order online (all major online retail sites carry our titles) or contact the distributor in the relevant country, listed on the copyright page.

See our website www.o-books.net for a full list of over 500 titles, growing by 100 a year.

And tune in to myspiritradio.com for our book review radio show, hosted by June-Elleni Laine, where you can listen to the authors discussing their books.

mySpiritRadio